The President's Pen: Reflections on Presidential Literature

Jeffrey A. Margolis

Great Day Bks LLC
Naples, FL

Photos courtesy of Library of Congress

ISBN: 978-1-62249-541-2

Published by
Biblio Publishing
Columbus, Ohio
BiblioPublishing.com

Great Day Bks LLC
5588 Hammock Isles Drive
Naples, FL 34119

www.presidentspen.com

DEDICATION

To Ida, my life partner, best friend, and fellow Presidential researcher

Also by Jeffrey A. Margolis

Teen Crime Wave: A Growing Problem (1997)

Violence in Sports: Victory at What Price? (1999)

Teens Who Kill (2000)

ACKNOWLEDGEMENTS

The research and review that is required for a book such as this cannot be done in a vacuum. In that regard I had a great deal of support and suggestions from several notable academics that I would like to thank. The late Dr. Fred Greenstein, professor emeritus from Princeton University's department of political science was the inspiration that gave me the idea of creating a book from my research. Although we had several brief meetings and one lunch together, his insight was most valuable. Another of his Princeton colleagues, Dr. Paul Miles, West Point graduate, Vietnam War veteran, and professor of history, has offered many suggestions and ideas that have been incorporated into this manuscript. Dr. Miles is a friend who has been most supportive of my efforts.

I would also like to acknowledge and thank Dr. June Sochen, professor emerita of history, Northeastern Illinois University. Our dialogue about this topic has been engaging and her insights have often led me down a research path that I had not previously thought of.

Many thanks to the researchers, librarians and archivists at the many presidential libraries and museums, who provided helpful suggestions and recommendations for my investigations. A special thanks to the excellent staff at the Herbert Hoover Presidential Library and Museum in West Branch, Iowa, and to the helpful staff at the Mudd Manuscript Library at Princeton University.

I would be remiss if I did not acknowledge and thank my editor, Carole Greene. Her expertise and suggestions have been most valuable in the preparation of this book for publication.

Contents

INTRODUCTION

The Constitution of the United States does not require that America's presidents be good writers. No requirements exist other than to be a natural born US citizen, be at least 35 years old, and have resided in the United States for at least 14 years. However, throughout the history of our republic, presidential aspirants, sitting presidents, and former presidents have seen fit to write about myriad topics, whether they were good at it or not. Four US presidents have won the Nobel Prize, but none of them won it for literature. One US president earned a Pulitzer Prize for his work (John F. Kennedy, *Profiles in Courage*), but many believe it was not his finest literary effort. Three presidents did win Grammy Awards for the spoken versions of their books (Carter, Clinton, Obama). America's first true presidential author was so concerned about how his writings would be received in his home colony of Virginia, that he initially had his book published in Paris without his name on it.

Two of the president-authors discussed in this book were generals, both graduates of the United States Military Academy at West Point. One of them, Ulysses S. Grant, sought the advice of the creator of Tom Sawyer and Huckleberry Finn to help him prepare his autobiography. The other, Dwight D. Eisenhower, chronicled his account of World War II in Europe along with the events that made him an international hero, eventually a college president and ultimately President of the United States.

Four of the writers are father-and-son presidents, the only such pairs in the history of our country. One father, George Herbert Walker Bush, eschewed writing his own biography. Instead, he chose noted author and historian Jon Meacham to pen his legacy. George W. Bush, the 43rd President of the United States, authored "*41*" – as a tribute to his father.

The most prolific of the presidential writers was Theodore Roosevelt, who wrote over forty volumes. According to some accounts, he would have been able to forge a successful career as a writer had he not chosen politics as his profession. Roosevelt's public career included serving as police commissioner of the City of New York, governor of New York State, assistant secretary of the navy, vice president and then on to the presidency.

Some of the authors chose to write as candidates for president, outlining their plans and goals for their administration should they be elected and to garner public support for their cause. Others reflected on their presidencies, careers, and lives in the form of memoirs, autobiographies, speeches and other collected writings. A third group preferred to write about subjects totally unrelated to politics and focused on such topics as the American West, personal faith, and success in the business world.

To be sure, some of the books have been ghostwritten and other authors have chosen to use co-writers, but the notion of presidential literature as a subset of American literature or history as literature should be investigated. This book will not focus on every book ever written by a president. There are well over 100. A list of many of these publications will be found in the Appendix. Nor will this analysis address a president's notes, papers, articles, or speeches that have been collated into book form, some of which take up twenty volumes or more. I have selected sixteen president-authors whose work I found of interest and will offer comments and reviews in the chapters that follow.

DID THE COLLEGE EXPERIENCE MAKE A DIFFERENCE?

Readers may wish to draw their own conclusions about this topic, but here is some basic information. Both the most prolific author (Theodore Roosevelt) and the only Pulitzer Prize winner (John F. Kennedy) were Harvard alums. What is even more ironic is that the first books of each started out as senior papers written while they were students at the university. The second largest number of books by a president was written by Jimmy Carter, a graduate of the United States Naval Academy—not an institution known for producing literary scholars. America's first legitimate author-president was Thomas Jefferson, who was a graduate of The College of William and Mary. His literary skills are showcased in the Declaration of Independence, and few could argue with the eloquence of that document.

How will we remember the writings of our presidents? Many of their works are out of print or are available mainly at antiquarian bookshops or at auctions. In this digital age, a number of presidential works are available as downloads or as "read-only" on personal devices. Readers and historians can only hope the collective memory of presidential literature will be preserved over time and these books will be available to anyone who wishes to read them. Who will be committed to be the caretakers of this legacy?

The more recent presidents have libraries and museums that are the repositories of their keepsakes. There are also antiquarian book collectors who possess signed first editions of historical significance. These collectors, too, are guardians of the legacy of presidential writers. Ultimately it should be "We the People" who will be the ones to read and remember the printed words of our leaders.

This is a tribute to those who helped frame and defend the Constitution of the United States, especially the First Amendment that gave them, and all of us, the right to a free press. That amendment was listed first for many reasons. We should take the time to look into the thinking of our presidents and to see what they had to say and why they wanted to publish their thoughts.

Chapter One
America's First True Author/President

(Library of Congress Prints and Photographic Division, LC_DIG pga 11392)

Thomas Jefferson
Born: April 13, 1743- Albemarle County, Virginia
Died: July 4, 1826- Monticello, Virginia
Third President of the United States
Term: 1801-1809
Wife: Martha Skelton
Political Party: Democratic-Republican
Undergraduate College: William and Mary

Thomas Jefferson, one of the College of William and Mary's most notable alums had a penchant for writing and reading. The author, (and future vice president and president,) who distinguished himself by penning the Declaration of Independence, also possessed the largest private library in the colonies. He was probably America's first significant bibliophile. His extensive book collection became the foundation of the Library of Congress. The British burned the library during the War of 1812. In the aftermath of the war, Jefferson sold his personal book collection of over 6000 volumes to the federal government and sent them to Washington to rebuild the library.

"One of the gems of his collection was the *Cyropaedia*, an interpretation of the Cyrus Cylinder written in cuneiform by King Cyrus of Persia in 539 B.C.E. In it is purported to be the first bill on human rights that had a great impact on Jefferson. Jefferson enjoyed writing, especially letters. It is estimated that during his lifetime he penned over 16,000 letters. Historians believe that Jefferson's correspondence was his greatest contribution as a former president."[1]

NOTES ON THE STATE OF VIRGINIA (1785)

Jefferson's primary work may be considered the first true book written by a United States President. He was serving his first term as the Governor of Virginia when this book was written. In *Notes on the State of Virginia,* Jefferson examines the history of the colony as well as its natural resources. The only book-length work by Jefferson to be published in his lifetime, "it is recognized today as the best single statement of Jefferson's principles, the best reflections of his wide-ranging tastes and talents." [2] "The Notes on Virginia is probably the most important scientific and political book written by an American before 1785."[3]

Notes on the State of Virginia has a complicated history. It was largely written in 1781 and had an initial run of 200 copies, which were first printed in Paris in 1785. They were to be for private distribution while Jefferson was abroad representing the United States as a diplomat. Prior to that, in 1784, Jefferson attempted to have some copies printed in Philadelphia shortly before he left for France. However, he thought the price for publication was too high.[4] One of the earliest recipients of a copy of Jefferson's book was John Adams, who, along with his wife Abigail, read the book while traveling from Calais to London. Adams wrote: "I thank you kindly for your book. It is our meditation all the day long. I cannot say much about it, but I think it will do its author and his country great Honour (sic)."[5] Benjamin Franklin was also in Paris with John Adams, and received a copy as well.[6]

In 1786, a trade edition was published in French. The first regularly published English edition, printed by John Stockdale, appeared in London in 1787.[7] While in France, Jefferson did present a copy to the Marquis de Lafayette. The first American edition finally appeared in 1788 and was distributed throughout the colonies. Jefferson, perhaps ironically, was concerned how his fellow gentlemen farmers in Virginia would view his feelings about the institution of slavery. He was a major slaveholder himself. *Notes on the State of Virginia* is both a compilation of data by Jefferson about the state's natural resources and economy, and his vigorous argument about the nature of the good society, which he believed was manifested in Virginia. Jefferson had wanted copies of the book distributed to all of the students at the College of William and Mary.

WHY THIS BOOK?

According to historian and author William Peden, editor of a 1982 edition of *Notes,* "The motivating impulse behind Jefferson's book was the desire of the French government to amass a body of pertinent information concerning the American states."[8]

Basically, the book was written as an atlas and gazetteer; Jefferson was responding to Francois Marbois, Secretary of the French legation in the Colonies, who had posed a series of queries about America and its resources. As such, *Notes on the State of Virginia* is comprised of chapters to answer those inquiries. They include a detailed description of the topography of Virginia, including the river known then as "Patowmac" now known as the Potomac (found in Query I). Other chapters address natural resources, trade, the location of Native American tribes, and the population of Virginia. But Jefferson chose to delve beyond creating a book of mere facts and figures. He includes a chapter on religion and religious freedom (Query xvii) and a lengthy discussion of the institution of slavery.

Jefferson was very conflicted about the "peculiar" institution of slavery. "He deplored the institution of slavery as unjust to its victims and injurious to the characters of its ostensible beneficiaries."[9] Jefferson did not believe that his own slaves were treated poorly. Yet he was one of the first to actually propose a detailed plan for emancipating slaves in Virginia. His plan called for freeing all the slaves born in Virginia after a specific date. He resented that the slaves were considered property—an issue that was not to be resolved for decades. But he was wary of the outcome of this progressive proposal. In *Notes* Jefferson believed that slavery was a "morally bankrupt institution, doomed to extinction and not compatible with the principles of the newly established United States of America.[10] He wrote: "Deep rooted prejudices entertained by the whites; ten thousand recollections, by the blacks, of the injuries they have sustained; new provocations; the real distinctions which nature has made; and many other circumstances, will divide us into parties, and produce convulsions which will probably never end but in the extermination of the one or the other race."[11]

Jefferson also had a great deal to say about religion, observing that Pennsylvania and New York offered religious freedom to citizens of all faiths. He wrote:

"...Their harmony is unparalleled, and can be ascribed to nothing but their unbounded tolerance, because there is no other circumstance in which they differ from every nation on earth."[12]

Peden went on to write: "In the *Notes* (on the state of Virginia), Jefferson at one time or another criticizes most of the vested interests of his time. He attacks the assumptions and usurpation of power by the rich, the powerful, and the well born; the tyranny of the church; the dogmas of the schoolmen; the bigotry of the man on horseback; the enslavement of man by man; the injustice of racial superiority." [13] Jefferson also takes the opportunity to mention immigration. "Here I will beg leave to propose a doubt. The present desire of America is to produce rapid population by as great importation of foreigners as possible. But is this founded in good policy?"[14]

The Massachusetts Historical Society owns the original manuscript of *Notes on the State of Virginia.* Prior to the book's publication, Jefferson reworked an earlier version of his manuscript by using sealing wax to attach to full handwritten pages his corrections and changes written on small additional pieces of paper. He also expanded the text by inserting additional full pages. These changes show the evolution of Jefferson's ideas on a number of topics, and the supplemental information he gathered as he wrote. In 1800 Jefferson wrote an appendix to his original manuscript with additional and updated information. In 1801 five new editions of *Notes on the State of Virginia* were published. By this time Jefferson was President of the United States and the opposition political party, the Federalists, were using some of the book's material for their own political purposes.[15]

THE JEFFERSON BIBLE **(1819)**

While Jefferson is best known for *Notes on the State of Virginia*, he did write other books, including an autobiography and book about the life of Jesus. This work, known as *The Jefferson Bible*, was written in 1819. Its original title was *The Life and Morals of Jesus of Nazareth*. It is Jefferson's interpretation of the life of Jesus.

"No man can conform his faith to the dictates of another. The life and essence of religion consists in the internal persuasion or belief of the mind." (Thomas Jefferson, 1819) Oddly, Jefferson never allowed the book to be published during his lifetime although he did show the manuscript to some of his friends. Beginning in 1904 and continuing every other year until the 1950s, new members of Congress were given a copy of *The Jefferson Bible.* Until the practice was stopped, the United States Government Printing Office provided the copies.

In January 2013, the American Humanist Association published an updated edition of *The Jefferson Bible*, and distributed a complimentary copy to every member of Congress as well as to President Barack Obama. The entire *Jefferson Bible* is available to view, page-by-page, on the Smithsonian National Museum of American History's website.

THE AUTOBIOGRAPHY OF THOMAS JEFFERSON **(1821)**

Three years before his death, at age seventy-seven, Jefferson penned his autobiography. Early chapters include his thoughts on the Articles of Confederation. He also chronicled his term as governor of

Virginia and his mission to France. Included in the autobiography are Jefferson's writings about his role as the first Secretary of State under President George Washington.

Jefferson writes about his ancestors and family who came to the Colonies from Wales. This book provides the reader with an accounting of Jefferson's younger life. He also writes about his time attending the College of William and Mary and entering the law profession. Jefferson discusses at length the Revolutionary War era and talks about the individuals he came in contact with, including John Adams and Benjamin Franklin, with whom he served in France. He ultimately recounts the story of his authoring the Declaration of Independence and those delegates who exacted wholesale changes in that most important document. He never forgave them. Jefferson used this 20-volume account to put forth his opinions about slavery, taxes, and even the death penalty.

Thomas Jefferson's other works encompassed a wide variety of topics. They included: *Observations of the Whaling Fisheries* (1788), *Manual for Parliamentary Practice* (1796), and the *History of the Expeditions of Lewis and Clark* (1814).

While many look to Jefferson's writing of the Declaration of Independence and his term as the third US President, as his greatest achievements, Jefferson himself believed that his greatest contribution was the establishment of the University of Virginia in Charlottesville and his contribution to the creation of a democratic republic that was to become known as the United States of America. Beyond that, Jefferson—the author— set the stage and a high standard for literary works of Presidents who came after him.

---

[1] Max J. Skidmore, *After the White House: Former Presidents as Private Citizens*
(New York: Palgrave MacMillan, 2004), 23.
[2] Thomas Jefferson, *Notes on the States of Virginia*, William Peden editor,
(New York: W.W. Norton and Company, 1954), v.
[3] *Ibid*.p. xi.
[4] Dumas Malone, *Jefferson and His Time, Vol.II. The Sage of Monticello*

(Boston: Little, Brown and Company, 1981), 94.
[5] Joseph Ellis. *American Sphinx: The Character of Thomas Jefferson* (New York: Vintage Press, 1998),101.
[6] *Ibid.*, p. 95.
[7] Peden, ed. p. v.
[8] Peden, ed. p. xi.
[9] Malone, p. 316.
[10] Ellis, p. 173.
[11] Peden, ed. p. 138.
[12] *Ibid.*, p. 161
[13] *Ibid.*, p. xxiii.
[14] *Ibid.*
[15] Ellis, p. 255.

CHAPTER TWO
THE HARVARD MEN

(Library of Congress, prints and photographic division, LOC pmsca 36434)

Theodore Roosevelt
Born- October 27, 1858- New York, New York
Died- January 6, 1919- Sagamore Hill, New York
26th President
Term: 1901-1909
Wife: Alice Lee, Edith Carow
Political Party: Republican
Undergraduate College- Harvard University
Nobel Peace Prize recipient- 1906

"Books are almost as individual as friends. There is no earthly use in laying down general laws about them. Some meet the needs of one person, and some of another; and each person should beware of the booklover's besetting sin, of what Mr. Edgar Allan Poe calls 'the mad pride of intellectuality,' taking the shape of arrogant pity for the man who does not like the same kind of books."

-Theodore Roosevelt.

Theodore Roosevelt was, by far, the most prolific writer of all the United States Presidents. He is credited with writing over 40 books. He began writing long before he entered politics, and it is widely believed that he could have made a living as a writer had his career not taken another direction. Why did Roosevelt write? In the early stages of his writing career, Roosevelt wrote for essentially two reasons: to earn money during difficult economic times, and to provide his readers with a portrait of the rugged outdoors life and the romance of the great American West.

Roosevelt's first book, *The Naval War of 1812,* was originally a term paper that he researched as a student at Harvard College. The book was completed after he graduated, in 1882, at the age of 23. *The Naval War* was critical of the US Navy and its preparedness for combat. In it Roosevelt chided President Thomas Jefferson for that lack of preparation. The book included details of events and places, meticulously footnoted. It also highlighted Roosevelt's interest in guns, armaments, and troop strength, as well as listing the names of military leaders.

In retrospect, it was not surprising that Roosevelt gravitated toward this topic beyond his first book. One of Roosevelt's favorite reads was *Influence of Sea Power Upon History* by Alfred Thayer Mahan, published in 1890. Noted author and historian Doris Kearns Goodwin observed: "His interest in the war had been sparked by a volume in the Porcellian Club (an exclusive men-only club at Harvard), by the reigning British authority on the subject, William James. Angered by the biased, boastful approach of the author, who appeared "afflicted with a hatred toward the Americans, Roosevelt searched out American historians of the war, only to find their accounts equally distorted by jingoism."[1]

*Note- the full title of the book is *The Naval War of 1812 or the History of the United States Navy During the Last War with Great Britain to which is appended the Account of the Battle of New Orleans*. (Originally published in 1882 and republished in 1902 by G.P. Putnam's Sons, New York)

MORE ABOUT *THE NAVAL WAR OF 1812*

Roosevelt's first book was unique in its focus. "*The Naval War* (book) was the first operational history of the conflict based upon extensive research in original sources. Of all of Theodore Roosevelt's work, this was the most acclaimed and had the most lasting impact."[2]

The book is full of meticulous details—names of officers on both sides, names of ships and their tonnage, number and types of guns, as well as statistics of those killed and wounded in each battle. Readers would learn the difference between a frigate and a corvette. The appendix contains precise details for mathematically determining the tonnage of a naval vessel. Further, the book was an in-depth review of naval engagements on Lake Erie, Lake Ontario, and the Atlantic. Roosevelt noted: "This war should be studied with unceasing diligence; the pride of the two peoples to which naval affairs are so generally familiar has cleared all the details and laid bare all the episodes, and through the sneers which the victors should have spared, merely out of care for their own glory, at every step can be seen that great truth there is only for those who know how to prepare it."[3]

In *The Naval War*, Roosevelt never missed an opportunity to take a shot at Thomas Jefferson and how he (according to TR) ruined the United States Navy. "But the only activity ever exhibited by Congress in materially increasing their navy, previous to the war, had been partially carrying out President Jefferson's ideas of having an enormous force of very worthless gunboats, a scheme whose wisdom was about on par with some of that statesman's political and military theories." [4]

In his discussion of the Battle of New Orleans (1815) toward the end of the book, Roosevelt noted: "While our navy had been successful, the war on land had been for us full of humiliation." [5]

While Roosevelt had disdain for Jefferson, he was quite laudatory of General Andrew Jackson. In some of the concluding remarks in the book, Roosevelt wrote:
"But the war had a dual aspect. It was partly a contest between the two branches of the English race, and partly a last attempt on the part of the Indian tribes to check the advance of the most rapidly growing one of these same two branches; and this last portion of the struggle, though attracting comparatively little attention, was really much the most far-reaching in its effect upon history."[6]

Realizing the significance and worth of Roosevelt's efforts, the Department of the Navy had authorized that a copy of the book be placed on board every ship in the US Navy and the book should be used as a text at the Naval War College. (Note-according to Commander Benjamin Armstrong, a professor at the United States Naval Academy, the course in American Naval History usually covers the War of 1812 in one to two class sessions, which makes the reading of Roosevelt's two volume set now impractical.)

Ironically, in the future, Roosevelt would be in a position to actually have an opportunity to impact naval operations, when in 1897 President William McKinley appointed him Assistant Secretary of the Navy. Four years later, Roosevelt would become Commander-in-Chief of all of the military when he became President of the United States upon McKinley's assassination. At that time, at age 42, he was the youngest president in American history. During his term in office, Roosevelt was able to assemble and launch "The Great White Fleet." He did not hesitate to send the US Navy to Latin America to enforce the 1904 Roosevelt Corollary to the Monroe Doctrine.

The Naval War of 1812 received outstanding reviews both in the United States and abroad. *The New York Times* noted that the book is: "… an excellent one in every respect and shows in so young an author the best promises for a good historian, fearless of statement, caution, endeavor to be impartial and a brisk and interesting way of telling events."[7]

Beyond the successful initial effort of *The Naval War of 1812*, Roosevelt's subsequent works can be placed in three categories: adventures, biographies, and history/ politics. *Hunting Trips of a Ranchman* was the initial installment of what was to become a trilogy of books on hunting and ranching. It was published in 1885. It was followed by *Ranch Life and the Hunting Trail* in 1888 and *The Wilderness Hunter* in 1893.[8] In *Hunting Trips*, Roosevelt writes of his trips through the Little Missouri River and the Dakotas. He goes into meticulous detail on his ventures, highlighting his love of the outdoors and animals. *The Wilderness Hunter* focused on the habits of the grizzly bear, and *Ranch Life* gave a vivid account of his encounters with a variety of hunting game. The 1902 edition, published by the Century Company, was illustrated by Frederic Remington. All of these books received favorable reviews, although Roosevelt was not entirely satisfied with his work. He said: "I wish I could make my writings touch a higher plane."[9] As Brander Matthews, the Columbia University professor and arbiter of Arts and Letters, wrote years later, Roosevelt's writings were invariably "Tinglingly alive, masculine and vascular."[10]

THE BIOGRAPHIES

In June 1887 Roosevelt began writing his fourth book, a biography of Gouvernor Morris, which turned out to be one of his more important works. Morris was a Revolutionary-era diplomat. The volume was to be a part of the American Statesmen Series. The book traced Morris' career in France and his efforts to save King Louis XVI and Marie Antoinette. Roosevelt completed this project in September of the same year. Authors of a series were given the option of receiving a $500 flat fee or a percentage of the profits earned by their book.

Theodore Roosevelt authored a biography of Senator Thomas Hart Benton- *The Western Expansionist.* Written by Roosevelt, this work, like the Gouvernor Morris book, became part of the American Statesmen Series. The series was edited by historian Torrey Morse and, in addition, Roosevelt included works by Henry Cabot Lodge and journalist Carl Schurz, who was active in the anti-slavery movement. "In Benton he [Roosevelt] vigorously praised Manifest Destiny, championed the union and lashed out against abolitionists. He supported Benton's anti-British stand on the Oregon Boundary Dispute of the 1840's."[11]

Author William Henry Harbaugh wrote in his book *TR, The Life and Times of Theodore Roosevelt*: *"The Life of Thomas Hart Benton* represented not more than three months of scholarship and three months of intense, but spasmodic, writing in the ranch house.... To produce such a work in a few months, with all its faults, required both basic knowledge and prior deliberation to which few men of his age and varied activities could aspire."[12] The Benton biography remained a popular book for twenty years. It should be noted that Thomas Hart Benton was also one of the senators that John F. Kennedy chose to write about in his book *Profiles in Courage*.

THE ROUGH RIDERS (1899)

"Credit should go with the performance of duty and not with what is very often the accident of glory."

– Theodore Roosevelt, *The Rough Riders.*

By most accounts, Roosevelt's second most popular book was his account of his escapades in Cuba and the Battle of San Juan Hill during the Spanish American War— *The Rough Riders*. In 1899, *Scribner's Magazine* had contracted for TR to write six articles about his exploits in Cuba during the Spanish- American War. He was to be paid $1000 for each article and, when completed, the articles were to be published as a book.[13]

This was a considerable sum for the time. The articles were based on a diary of Roosevelt's experiences from the time he left America's shores until his triumphant return. The stories were eventually tied together and published as a book. Like many of Roosevelt's other offerings, *The Rough Riders* goes into the meticulous details of the Battle of San Juan Hill and his role in the battle. Edmund Morris, who wrote the introduction to one of the editions of the book, said: "Theodore Roosevelt assembled an improbable regiment of Ivy Leaguers, cowboys, Native Americans, African-Americans, and Western Territory land speculators."[14]

Peter Dunne, a columnist for *The Chicago Times-Herald* who used the pen name Martin Dooley, wrote a "book review" that appeared in *Harper's Weekly* and "mocked Roosevelt's propensity for placing himself at the center of all the action. He believed that the book should have been titled "Alone in Cuba."[15] According to another reviewer, Roosevelt was a major proponent of Manifest Destiny and was spoiling for a war. He said: "I should welcome any war. The country needs one."[16] He got his wish and a boost in popularity as well.

THE WINNING OF THE WEST (1889-96)

Roosevelt had completed his biography series and was seeking to produce a more substantial work. He said: "My literary work occupies a good deal of my time; and I have done fairly well at it. I should like to write some book that would really rank in the very first class."[17]

For some time he had been thinking about writing a multivolume history of the North American Continent- a sweeping drama of heroism, hardship, warfare and struggle."[18] And so in 1888, Roosevelt began work on what was to become his epic, *The Winning of the West*, which, completed, comprised four volumes. He was hoping that this effort would allow him to be taken seriously as an historian.

The Winning of the West provided Roosevelt with the literary and financial success he was so earnestly seeking. He was applauded for pointing out that a "new composite nationality... a distinct American people" had emerged beyond the Alleghenies. The book was a major contribution to the narrative history of the West. A generation of Americans eagerly devoured it.[19]

"*The Winning of the West* remains one of the greatest works of western history . . . [It] reflects the character of its author. It is sometimes quirky and full of prejudices and blind spots, but it is cultivated and sweeping in its learning and encompassing in its judgments." -John Milton Cooper Jr. Dr. Cooper is a Pulitzer Prize winning historian and professor emeritus at the University of Wisconsin-Madison.

(Author's Note- The original handwritten manuscript of volume one of *The Winning of the West* is currently located at the New York Public Library.)

HISTORY AS LITERATURE AND OTHER ESSAYS (CHARLES SCRIBNER'S SONS. 1913)

With meticulous detail and explanation, Theodore Roosevelt makes the case for the importance of history that can be viewed through the scientific as well as the literary lens. He notes "writings are useless unless they are read and they cannot be read unless they are readable." *History as Literature* was written in 1913 and presented at a conference of the American Historical Society, when Roosevelt firmly established himself as a legitimate and thoughtful historian. Although his total body of written work includes his adventures and biographies, from his initial publication of *The Naval Battles of the War of 1812* to the 1918 *National Strength and International Duty*, Theodore Roosevelt has proven to his readers that he is a legitimate historical author.

In the preface of this work, written after he left the White House, Roosevelt observes: "In these addresses and essays I have discussed not merely literary but also historical and scientific subjects, for my thesis is that the domain of literature must be ever more widely extended over the domains of history and science."

Roosevelt's *History as Literature and Other Essays* is a book in the literal sense but was essentially a collection of the former president's addresses and essays presented at the University of Oxford, the Sorbonne, the University of Berlin and the American Historical Association. Included in this anthology are works previously published by "*The Outlook*," (a magazine of which Roosevelt was a staff member) and *The Century*, which had previously published some of the writings of Ulysses S. Grant.

Roosevelt continued to write both during and well after his presidency. His topics still spotlighted his love for adventure and travel (*Through the Brazilian Wilderness*- 1914) but also included his passion for history (*America and the World War*-1915) and a more somber National Strength and International Duty (1917).

Roosevelt's last major work, *The Great Adventure: Present Day Studies in American Nationalism,* was published in 1918. *The Great Adventure* was dedicated to "all who in this war have paid with their bodies for their souls' desire." He begins the work with this philosophical observation: "Only those who are fit to live who do not fear to die; and are fit to die who had shrunk from the joy of life and the duty of life. Both life and death are part of the same great adventure."[20] Ever the politician, Roosevelt urged his readers to repudiate President Woodrow Wilson's fourteen points and wrote of his disdain for Wilson. Six months after the book's publication

Roosevelt would be dead, bringing to an end a remarkable political as well as literary life.

ROOSEVELT AS MAGAZINE WRITER

In addition to the many books Roosevelt had penned, he also wrote for a number of periodicals. They included *Harper's Monthly Magazine* and the *Ladies Home Journal.*

In the Journal, Roosevelt "urged men to engage in civic activity and be good family men."[21] He was also known to write letters to magazines, especially women's magazines.

He loved to travel. "His travels were valuable and he made an immensely favorable impression throughout Europe. Instead of the rude frontier manners that many Europeans expected from Americans, they found the former president to be skilled in French, German, and Italian and [have] wide literary and historical knowledge."[22] His well-traveled life only served to enhance his literary skills, skills that were germinated long before he reached Harvard.

Roosevelt remains today the consummate presidential writer and historian. He was the first president elected in the twentieth century and the first to use photographs in newspapers and magazines to chronicle his accomplishments. He was the president of many "firsts." Roosevelt was the president who built the Panama Canal. "TR was the first president to go down in a submarine, the first to go up in an airplane, the first to call it the White House, officially. Most importantly, he saw himself as a world leader."[23] He was also the first president to earn the Nobel Peace Prize.

Theodore Roosevelt possessed an intellectual curiosity for just about everything and had a lifelong interest in communicating his findings to his readers. His books were the vehicles for sharing his findings with the world.

(Library of Congress print and photographic Division, LC-USZ62-13035)

John Fitzgerald Kennedy - thirty-fifth President of the United States
Born- May 29, 1917- Brookline, Massachusetts
Died- November 22, 1963- Dallas, Texas
Term: January 1961-November 1963
Wife: Jacqueline Bouvier
Political Party- Democratic
Undergraduate College- Harvard University

"A man does what he must — in spite of personal consequences, in spite of obstacles and dangers, and pressures — and that is the basis of all human morality."

- John F. Kennedy, *Profiles in Courage*

John F. Kennedy had the gift of being both an eloquent speaker and a good writer. He also had the good fortune of being born into a family that could help him achieve his personal and professional aspirations. As Kennedy was one of five US Presidents to graduate from Harvard College, it can be noted that the university assuredly fulfilled its mission to "educate the citizens and citizen-leaders for our society."

Even before his writing and political career, Kennedy was an avid reader of a wide selection of titles whose content helped to shape some of his future thinking. They included *Uncle Tom's Cabin* by Harriet Beecher Stowe, *Pilgrim's Progress* by John Bunyon and, ironically, *King Arthur and the Round Table* by A.M. Hadfield (fr. Rose Kennedy Personal Papers). Even into his presidency, Kennedy continued to read, this time with a more marked historical interest.

Some of the books he read included *John Quincy Adams* by Samuel Flagg Bemis, *The Price of Union* by Herbert Agar, and *The Emergence of Lincoln* by Allan Nevins. Nevins went on to become editor of several of Kennedy's later works.[24] (White House Central Subject Files, Box 722)

KENNEDY AS JOURNALIST

John Kennedy was discharged from the Navy in April of 1945 after recuperating from injuries sustained during World War II. He immediately went to work as a reporter for the International News Service. One of his assignments was to cover the initial meeting of the newly formed United Nations in San Francisco, California. In July of that year Kennedy was dispatched to Paris on special assignment by the Hearst Newspapers organization. He was also asked by his family to serve as editor of a limited-edition book that was to be a tribute to his late brother, Joseph P. Kennedy Jr., a navy pilot who was killed in action over England during World War II. One hundred fifty copies of *As We Remember Joe* were distributed to family and friends.

The thirty–fifth President of the United States, Kennedy is best remembered for his speeches, most notably his Inaugural Address and his stirring "Ich bin ein Berliner" speech in West Berlin on June 26, 1963. Kennedy is also remembered for his glib comments at his press conferences. Most Americans are less familiar with his writings. Kennedy was the author of six books, two of which were written before he became President of the United States. His second book, *Profiles in Courage*, garnered him a Pulitzer Prize. But his first literary effort, *Why England Slept*, merits the reader's attention. Although not as serious a student as Theodore Roosevelt, Kennedy, at age 22, took a page out of TR's playbook by reworking his senior honors thesis at Harvard into a complete book. The thesis was originally titled "Appeasement at Munich." In Kennedy's case, he had resources from his father, Joseph P. Kennedy, who was serving as the Ambassador to the Court of St. James at the time and whose office was able to provide statistical information to support Kennedy's thesis. Mona Brown, an assistant to the ambassador, transcribed the manuscript for Kennedy.

During the year prior to writing his paper, Kennedy took a leave from Harvard and traveled overseas, visiting Germany, France, Poland, Latvia, Turkey, Russia, and even Palestine. Armed with this first-hand information, he began to write about the conditions he discovered in Europe. The trip served to help him focus on his project.

Why England Slept examines the thinking of the British government under Prime Minister Neville Chamberlain and why the country was unprepared to go to war against Hitler. The book examines the British policy of appeasement of the Nazi regime. Why was England so slow to re-arm prior to World War II? Kennedy points to the fact that democracies proceed at a much slower pace than dictatorships. It is well known now that the policy of appeasement did little to stop German aggression. The United States, too, it should be noted, took its time to move from isolationism to become the leader of the Allied forces. The book is subtitled "The inevitable result of the slowness of conversion of the British Democracy from a disarmament to a rearmament policy." (Dated March 15, 1940.)

The text is divided into three parts:
Part I- the Period of Disarmament Policy
Part II- The Period of Rearmament Policy
Part III- Conclusion

Kennedy's thesis advisor, Carl J. Friedrich, professor of government at Harvard, commented: "Much too long, wordy, repetitious… Yet, thesis shows real interest and reasonable amount of work, though labor of condensation would have helped. Many typographical errors. English diction defective."[25]

Kennedy viewed his work as an answer to *While England Slept*, written by Winston Churchill two years before his book. JFK's book initially sold 80,000 plus copies in the United States and the United Kingdom and became a bestseller. Joseph P. Kennedy, John's father, was instrumental in getting the book published and reportedly sent a copy to Winston Churchill. But critics point to Kennedy's privileged upbringing that helped pave the way for the book's publication. "His senior theses also reflected Kennedy's elite advantages, including professional stenographic, dictation and typing and editorial assistance from such journalistic notables as Arthur Krock and Henry Luce."[26] Krock was a close friend of JFK's father, Joseph P. Kennedy, and was a columnist for *The New York Times*. He believed that Kennedy's project was worthy of publication. He helped edit and revise the literary style and came up with the title. Another review concluded: "Its analysis was grounded in the lesson of history and reflected a whiggish cast of mind that lamented the slowness and uncertainties of democracies when threatened by authoritarian regimes."[27]

Why England Slept, as it was titled when published in 1940, came to press well before Pearl Harbor and the US entry into World War II. It was reissued in 1961 during Kennedy's presidency. John Kennedy dedicated the book to his parents, Rose and Joseph P. Kennedy. For some reason, copies of *Why England Slept*, which has been out of print, are often hard to obtain, even in antiquarian circles. Recently a signed first-edition (with dust jacket) was for sale in a Las Vegas bookshop for about $11,000. In 2019, a signed first edition, with dust jacket, was featured in a rare book catalogue for $25,000.

PROFILES IN COURAGE

Profiles in Courage is Kennedy's best-known work. The idea for the book came to Kennedy in 1954, and he worked on the manuscript while convalescing from serious back surgery in Boston. In his query letter to Cass Canfield, chairman of the board at Harper and Brothers Publishers in 1955, Kennedy proposed a working title of "Patterns of Political Courage."[28] However, in a note to his sister Eunice, he proposed four other possible titles: Men of Courage, Eight Were Courageous, Call the Roll, and Profiles of Courage. Harper was suggesting a book length of between forty thousand and sixty thousand words. Kennedy had begun to narrow the focus of his work to be limited exclusively to United States Senators who exhibited the courage of their convictions during crucial times in American history.

As a freshman senator from Massachusetts, Kennedy examines eight of his predecessors in Congress, including John Quincy Adams, whose senate seat Kennedy held. Kennedy took an introspective look at these eight remarkable men and how they succeeded with their convictions despite being faced with opposition. The men he chose to write about were resolute and displayed extraordinary courage. "Great crises produce great men and great deeds of courage." [29]

One of Senator Kennedy's choices to write about was Senator Thomas Hart Benton. Fellow President/author Theodore Roosevelt had written an entire biography about Benton in 1886. Other senators who fit into Kennedy's template of courage included Daniel Webster, Sam Houston and Edmund Ross, who was singled out for his pivotal vote in the impeachment of President Andrew Johnson which led to Johnson's acquittal.

On May 7, 1957, Kennedy received a letter from John Hohenberg at Columbia University informing him that he had been awarded the Pulitzer Prize for Biography. Included in the letter was a check for $500. Kennedy donated his prize money to the United Negro College Fund. *Profiles in Courage* was also a National Book Award finalist for non-fiction.

There have been numerous editions of *Profiles in Courage* printed since the original publication in 1957. A special edition was published in 1961 to commemorate the inauguration of John F. Kennedy. A special memorial edition was printed after his assassination. A forward to that edition was written by the President's brother, Robert F. Kennedy, on December 18, 1963, less than a month after JFK's death. A 2003 edition includes an Introduction by Kennedy's daughter, Caroline Kennedy. *Profiles in Courage* is the only book written by a US President that was selected by the prestigious Chautauqua Institution as one of their selections of the Literary and Scientific Circle. During its initial release, the book remained on the bestseller list for ninety-five weeks. In 1964, *Profiles in Courage* was made into a television series with 26 episodes produced.

In his book, *The Audacity of Hope*, Barack Obama quoted this passage from *Profiles in Courage*: "Few, if any, face the dread finality of decision that confronts a Senator facing an important call of the roll. He may want more time for his decision - he may believe there is something to be said for both sides - he may feel that a slight amendment could remove all difficulties-but when that roll is called he cannot hide, he cannot equivocate, he cannot delay - and he senses that his constituency, like the Raven in Poe's poem, is perched there on his Senate desk, croaking 'Nevermore' as he casts the vote that stakes his political future."[30]

GHOSTWRITER CONTROVERSY

Soon after the publication of *Profiles in Courage*, Mike Wallace of CBS News interviewed writer Drew Pearson. Pearson stated that the book was essentially ghostwritten by Kennedy's aide and speechwriter, Theodore Sorensen. In the final published version, Kennedy inserted a handwritten sentence acknowledging Sorensen's contribution. It reads: "The greatest debt is owed to my research assistant Theodore C. Sorensen for his invaluable assistance in the assembly and preparation of the material upon which this book is based."[31]

In his own autobiography, *Counselor: a Life at the Edge of History*, Sorensen acknowledged that he did much of the research for the book and wrote most of the first draft. Unfortunately, Sorensen received none of the accolades that went with the book's Pulitzer Prize award. Herbert Parmet, distinguished history professor at City University of New York, also investigated the incubation of *Profiles in Courage*. He concluded:

> "The research, tentative drafts and organization were left to the collective labor of others, and the literary craftsmanship was clearly the work of Ted Sorensen."[32]

REVIEW OF *PROFILES IN COURAGE*

Henry Luce, editor-in-chief of *Time Magazine*, wrote the introduction to *Profiles in Courage*. He said: "If John Kennedy is characteristic of the younger generation- and I believe he is—many of us would be happy to have the destinies of the Republic handed over to his generation at once."[33] Many believed that this was the book that could launch Kennedy into the national spotlight. In his book, *The Letters of John F. Kennedy*, author Martin Sandler wrote: "In the opinion of many political pundits, the national attention and acclaim he (Kennedy) received from the publication of *Profiles in Courage* truly set him on the road to the White House."[34]

THE LEGACY OF *PROFILES IN COURAGE*

Several projects have germinated from *Profiles in Courage* since its original publication. The John. F. Kennedy Library Foundation established the Profile in Courage Award given to "an individual who displays the kind of exemplary political courage and integrity described in the book." Both Presidents George H.W. Bush and Barack Obama have been recipients of this award. The Library Foundation also founded The John F. Kennedy Profile in Courage Essay Contest. The program encourages school students from around the United States to write an essay about an elected official at the local, state or national level who is acting courageously to deal with a current issue of political importance. This contest is open to all US high school students in grades nine through twelve in public, private, or parochial schools as well as students who are home- schooled. For more information, those interested can access information at www.jfkcontest.org.

In 2002, Caroline Kennedy, JFK's daughter, wrote and edited *Profiles in Courage for Our Time,* which examines more recent American heroes.

A NATION OF IMMIGRANTS (1958)

"The interaction of disparate cultures, the vehemence of the ideals that led the immigrants here, the opportunity offered by a new life, all gave America a flavor and a character that make it as unmistakable and as remarkable to people today as it was to Alexis de Tocqueville in the early part of the nineteenth century."

-John F. Kennedy, *A Nation of Immigrants*

Kennedy's final book, *A Nation of Immigrants*, may be a most timely book for today.

Originally written in 1958, when Kennedy was still a US senator from Massachusetts, the book examines the waves of immigrants who arrived on our shores at different times in our history from diverse parts of the globe for a wide variety of reasons. It provides the reader with a chronology of the immigration story in America. It emphasizes the importance of immigration and the rise and success of the United States of America and how our nation has thrived as a result. Kennedy was seeking a platform from which to make public his feelings and beliefs for a sound immigration policy in this country. He noted that in the course of the history of the United States, 42 million immigrants came to America's shores.

As the immigration debate in this country continues, *A Nation of Immigrants* would be quite relevant today, defining what a sound and responsible immigration policy should look like. Considering that Kennedy was the descendant of Irish immigrants, his prose was an impassioned examination of the immigrant experience. His position: Unless you were on the shore welcoming the Pilgrims at Plymouth, you're an immigrant. In his writings, Kennedy addresses the issue of xenophobia in America and how it was impacting official immigration policy. He believed that the concept of "America" was a grand experiment with a vast "melting pot" of new arrivals eager to become part of that experiment. Kennedy also addresses the issue of discrimination and how that "grand experiment" of American democracy failed the African-American community.

In *A Nation of Immigrants*, Kennedy examines several of the most notable groups to arrive on America's shores. Most immigrant groups came for a variety of reasons: for better economic conditions, to flee religious persecution or to escape political unrest. It did not matter that they did not know the language or facts about American culture.

Kennedy points out that the issue of immigration is not a new one. As far back as 1797, there had been a movement in Congress to stop immigration.[35]

Kennedy was passionate about immigration throughout his time in office. In a letter written on March 13,1961, to Angier Biddle DukePresident of The American Immigration and Citizenship Conference, Kennedy wrote: "Our immigration programs must be free from any taint of racism or discrimination. We must never forget that we are a nation of immigrants, and that our land has always been, and must continue to be, a haven for the persecuted and oppressed who seek the air of freedom."[36]

John Kennedy had a longstanding relationship with the Anti-Defamation League (ADL) that began when he was a junior senator from Massachusetts. He had written two articles that appeared in the ADL bulletin, one in February 1959, and the other, that was taken from the text of a speech Kennedy delivered, in January 1961.

In 1958 the ADL had asked the first-term senator from Massachusetts to write an essay about immigration. Sol Kolack, the Regional Director of ADL New England, asked Kennedy to develop a manuscript "on the matter of immigration and on the contribution of immigrants to the greatness of our nation." The Anti-Defamation

League originally published A *Nation of Immigrants* as part of a series entitled "One Nation Library." Kennedy went on to revise his essay into a complete book.

In 1961 President Kennedy was the keynote speaker at the ADL annual meeting and again in January 1963, where he received the ADL's America's Democratic Legacy Award for his commitment to immigration reform in the United States. In August 1963, excerpts were published in *The New York Times Magazine*. A complete edition of the book was published in 1964, with an introduction by JFK's brother, Robert F. Kennedy.

Abraham Foxman, national director of the Anti-Defamation League, wrote the introduction to the original edition. Praise for the book came from all corners of America. (Note- the first edition of this book included a full-color-folding map inside the rear cover.) The ADL owned the original copyright to the book and still does today.

It is the material contained in the last two chapters of *Nation of Immigrants* that Kennedy was hoping to use to refocus American immigration policy and advocate for substantive changes. Unfortunately, Kennedy was assassinated prior to the book's completion and A *Nation of Immigrants* was published posthumously.

In addition to signing civil rights legislation, President Lyndon Johnson wished to continue the legacy of Kennedy's book by signing the Immigration and Nationality Act in New York on October 3, 1965. This legislation, originally introduced by Senator Philip Hart of Michigan, (S.747), was one of the most comprehensive changes to immigration law in this country's history. It sought to level the immigration playing field and remove racial quotas.

In the original edition of *A Nation of Immigrants*, Kennedy provided a chronology of immigration in America beginning with the 1607 founding of the Virginia Colony and concluding with Kennedy's request to the Congress in 1963 to enact new immigration legislation that would eliminate quotas based on national origin.

In the most recent edition in 2018, an additional appendix was added after Kennedy's assassination. This supplement begins with President Johnson signing the 1965 act that liberalized immigration policies that Kennedy sought. The supplement goes up to May 2018, when then US Attorney General Jeff Sessions announced his "zero tolerance policy toward refugees crossing the US-Mexico border."

Much of the message of the book is still relevant today. *A Nation of Immigrants* is one standout presidential work that had a direct impact on federal government policy at that time.

REVIEW OF *A NATION OF IMMIGRANTS*

High praise was given for *A Nation of Immigrants.* In a review by Jesse Gordon of *On the Issues,* he wrote: "This book should be read by every politician involved in the immigration debate, and by every citizen interested in the current immigration debate- which means it should be read by every American."[37] Florida Senator Marco Rubio wrote: "An enduring reminder of where we—the United States of America—come from. We must remain mindful that there is much more that unites us than divides us.... John F. Kennedy's legacies are many, but let *A Nation of Immigrants* always remind us of our shared dreams, goals, and destiny as a nation."

Dr. Andrew Roth, Scholar-in-Residence at the Jefferson Educational Society, noted that Kennedy firmly believed that America was truly a nation of immigrants. "He believed as I do, that it is possible to become one people committed to America's ideals while still maintaining a sense of pride in one's ethnic heritage."[38]

There are three other books attributed to John F. Kennedy. They are *The Strategy of Peace* (1961), *To Turn the Tide* (1962), and *The Burden and the Glory* (1964). Noted historian Allan Nevins edited two of these books. These works are essentially collections of speeches and policy addresses made by Kennedy between 1957 and 1959 during his presidential run. Much of his vision was spot on and relevant, even today. He addressed the issues of nuclear arms, climate change, the Middle East, and Vietnam.

THE STRATEGY OF PEACE (1960)

As a US Senator, Kennedy published *The Strategy of Peace* in 1960 as he was preparing his run for the presidency. Edited by Allan Nevins, this book is comprised of foreign policy speeches and comments that covered a wide spectrum of issues on foreign policy, world peace, national defense and security. Kennedy believed that the United States must be the leader on the world stage and be willing to negotiate with its adversaries. One of the notable inclusions in this work was Kennedy's remarks to the graduating class of American University on June 10, 1960.

"Our problems are man-made. Therefore, they can be solved by man. And man can be as big as he wants. No problem of human destiny is beyond human beings. Man's reason and spirit have often solved the seemingly unsolvable—and we believe they can do it again. ... In the final analysis, our most basic common link is that we all inhabit this small planet. We all breathe the same air. We all cherish our children's future. And we are all mortal."

THE BURDEN AND THE GLORY (1964)

The Burden and the Glory includes the speech that Kennedy was scheduled to give in Dallas on November 22, 1963. After the assassination, editor Allan Nevins brought together addresses and public statements, as well as new material that highlights the President's views on civil rights, America's goals in science and education, the Cuban Missile Crisis, and the efforts toward a nuclear test ban treaty. Nevins, himself a two-time Pulitzer Prize winner and noted Columbia University history professor, was a long-time friend of Kennedy. Also included in this volume is Kennedy's memorable "Ich Ben Ein Berliner" speech. President Lyndon Johnson wrote the forward to this book.

KENNEDY AND HIS LETTERS

John F. Kennedy was an avid letter writer. He apparently enjoyed communicating with friends, heads of state, and many notables, including sports figures like Jackie Robinson and icons like the Reverend Billy Graham. Early in his presidential campaign Kennedy received many letters questioning his ability to serve as president while being a practicing Catholic. His responses were always to the point, affirming his belief in separation of church and state as delineated in the US Constitution. There were also a number of letters between Kennedy and poet Robert Frost. Kennedy held Frost and his work in high regard and invited him to read an original poem at his inauguration. Most notable, however, is a series of letters between Kennedy and former First Lady Eleanor Roosevelt. Mrs. Roosevelt expressed a great deal of disdain for the Kennedy family, especially Joseph P. Kennedy, the president's father. The former First Lady intimated that the father was "buying" the presidency for his son. Kennedy was ever the diplomat in his responses and went on to have a cordial relationship with Mrs. Roosevelt.

As Martin Sandler, editor of the book *The Letters of John F. Kennedy* noted: "Yet, for all of John Kennedy's good looks and telegenic charm, at his core he was a reader and a writer. Indeed, he was among the best-read and most articulate presidents the United States has ever had." The only other recent president who possessed those skills was Barack Obama.

Given Kennedy's adeptness for both speaking and writing, it is not difficult to imagine that he would have continued to write more had his life not been snuffed out at such an early age. Kennedy was not the first president to write books, but his literary works have become a rich part of his legacy.

---

[1] Doris Kearns Goodwin, *The Bully Pulpit: Theodore Roosevelt, William Howard Taft and the Gilded Age of Journalism* (New York: Simon and Schuster, Inc., 2013), 65.
[2] Nathan Miller, *Theodore Roosevelt- A Life* (New York: William Morrow, 1992),116.
[3] Theodore Roosevelt, The Naval War of 1812
(New York: Modern Library, 1999 edition),75.
[4] *Ibid.*, p. 246.
[5] *Ibid.*, p. 251.
[6] *Ibid.*, p. 252
[7] Miller, p.129.
[8] William Henry Harbaugh, *The Life and Times of Theodore Roosevelt*
(New York: Collins Books, 1961), 55.
[9] *Ibid.*, p. 56.
[10] *Ibid.*
[11] Miller, p. 180.
[12] Harbaugh, p. 58.
[13] Miller, p. 316.
[14] Edmund Morris, reported in *Goodreads*, accessed 9/15/19.
[15] Goodwin, pp. 257-258

[17] Goodwin, p. 129.
[18] Miller, p. 197.
[19] *Ibid.*, p. 200.
[20] Theodore Roosevelt, *The Great Adventure: Present Day Studies in American Nationalism (*New York: Charles Scribner's Sons, *1918), 1.*
[21] John W. Matviko,ed. *The American President in Popular Culture* (Westport, Connecticut: Greenwood Press, 2005), 126.
[22] Skidmore, p. 96.
[23] David McCullough. *The American Spirit: Who we are and What we Stand For*
(New York: Simon & Schuster, 2017). 67

[24] White House Central Subject Files, Box 722
[25] From John F. Kennedy Library and Museum- accessed July 18,2019
[26]*Ibid*, p. 638.
[27]Kathryn Moore, *American Presidents*: *A Complete History* (New York: Fall River Press, 2007), 637.
[28] Martin Sandler, ed. *The Letters of John F. Kennedy* (New York: Bloomsbury Press. 2013). 46.
[29] John F. Kennedy. *Profiles in Courage* (New York: Harper Brothers. 1956), 51.
[30] Barack Obama. *The Audacity of Hope: Thoughts on Reclaiming the American Dream.* (New York: Crown Publishers. 2006), 129.
[31] John F. Kennedy Library and Museum. Accessed July, 19, 2019
[32] Tevi Troy. *What Jefferson Read, Ike Watched, and Obama Tweeted* (Washington, D.C.: Regnery Publishing, Inc., 2010), 188.
[33] Sandler, p. 4.
[34] *Ibid.*, p. 45.
[35] John F. Kennedy. *A Nation of Immigrants* (New York: Harper Perennial, 2018). 37-40.
[36] Sandler, p. 189.
[37] Jesse Gordon. Book Review-On The Issues.org. July 2012. Accessed July 18, 2018
[38] Conversation with Andrew Roth, July 8,2019, Chautauqua Institution

Chapter Three
The West Point Presidents

(Library of Congress print and Photographic Division, loc-usz62-13018)

Ulysses S. Grant
Born: April 27, 1822- Point Pleasant, Ohio
Died: July 23, 1885- Wilton, New York
18th President of the United States
Term: 1869-1877
Wife: Julia Dent
Political Party: Republican
Undergraduate College: United States Military Academy

Twelve US presidents have served as generals in the United States Army. (See Appendix II for a complete list.) Only two of them, Ulysses S. Grant and Dwight D Eisenhower, were graduates of the United States Military Academy at West Point. Both men went on to be outstanding military leaders and then on to the presidency without holding any other political office. Both Grant and Eisenhower were Republicans. Grant initially did not want to go to the military academy. His father had applied for his appointment and Grant initially said he would not attend. Even when he arrived at West Point, he was hoping that Congress would abolish the academy as it was threatening to do in 1839. "A military life had no charms for me, and I had not the faintest idea of staying in the army even if I should be graduated, which I did not expect."[1] As Grant became more acclimated to military life and the course work, he sometimes mused about becoming a mathematics professor there and later moving on to teach at a college. Grant's middling class rank—he graduated number 21 in a class of 39 cadets—limited his choices as to which branch of the Army to serve. Even today class rank still helps determine a cadet's branch, such as infantry, artillery, or cavalry.[2] Upon his graduation, Grant had sought to enter the cavalry but ended up as an infantry officer.

PERSONAL MEMOIRS OF ULYSSES S. GRANT

Ulysses S. Grant wrote only one book during his lifetime, his *Personal Memoirs*. The two-volume work traces his life from his youth to his days at West Point. Other chapters examine his life during the Mexican-American War and ultimately as a general in the Civil War. The first of two volumes were originally published on December 10, 1885.

The memoir has been highly regarded by the public, military historians and literary critics. Grant portrayed himself in the persona of the honorable Western hero, whose strength lies in his honesty and straightforwardness. He candidly depicted his battles against both the Confederates and internal army foes. The book is consistently mentioned as one of the ten best books ever written by a US president.

Mark Twain called *Memoirs* a "literary masterpiece." Given over a century of favorable literary analysis, reviewer Mark Perry states that the Memoirs are "the most significant work" of American non-fiction. "Man proposes and God disposes," wrote Grant. "There are but few important events in the affairs of men brought about by their own choice. Although frequently urged by friends to write my memoirs, I had determined never to do so, nor to write anything for publication. In preparing these volumes for the public, I have entered upon the task with the sincere desire to avoid doing injustice to anyone, whether on the National or Confederate side, other than the unavoidable injustice of not making mention often where special mention is due."[3]

In *Personal Memoirs*, Grant revisits his youth and career at the United States Military Academy (West Point). He noted that he learned a great deal about battlefield tactics and leadership from General Zachary Taylor during the Mexican-American War (1846).

Grant's military philosophy was not fanciful. "The art of war is simple enough. Find out where your enemy is. Get at him as soon as you can. Strike him as hard as you can and as often as you can and keep moving on." Conspicuously missing from the work are any discussions of his marriage, his family, his trip around the world or his presidency.

"Resisting postwar cries for revenge, Grant refused to exult in the 'downfall' of his enemies, yet he also refused to exalt the rebels, no matter how 'long and valiantly'
they battled and no matter 'the sincerity with which they suffered for their morally bankrupt enterprise.'"[4]

Grant's memoirs contain 79 chapters with a significant number of maps and charts. He goes into great detail about the Mexican War and the annexation of Texas. At that time, he served under the command of General Zachary Taylor mentioned above.
Upon learning about the Confederate attack on Fort Sumter, South Carolina, on April 11, 1860, Grant remarked that it was "...an insult to the national flag."[5]

Personal Memoirs details the critical Civil War battles of Shiloh, Chattanooga, Vicksburg and Spotsylvania. He candidly discusses learning about his appointment as brigadier-general by President Lincoln by reading a St. Louis newspaper. Grant discusses the key players in his military successes and triumphs in these Civil War battles. Readers can gain Grant's perspectives on battlefield decision-making, and his role as both a leader and tactician.

Grant spends a great deal of time discussing the siege of Vicksburg, replete with maps, charts and meticulous details with names of opposing generals, amount of armaments, as well as casualty lists. "The fate of the Confederacy was sealed when Vicksburg fell. Much hard fighting was to be done afterwards and many precious lives were to be sacrificed; but the morale was with the supporters of the Union ever after."[6]

ABOUT THE AUTHOR

As Commanding General of the United States Army (1864-69), Grant was handpicked by President Lincoln and worked closely with him to lead the Union Army to victory over the Confederacy in the Civil War. "General Grant, the nation's appreciation of what you have done, and its reliance upon you for what remains to be done in the existing great struggle, are now presented, with this commission constituting you Lieutenant-General in the Army of the United States. With this high honor devolves upon you also a corresponding responsibility as the country herein trusts you so, under God, it will sustain you." (President Abraham Lincoln to U.S. Grant, March 9, 1864)[7]

As the youngest president of the nineteenth century, Grant implemented Congressional Reconstruction, often at odds with the policies of Lincoln's successor, Andrew Johnson. Elected to two terms as president, Grant led the Republican Party in their effort to remove the remnants of Confederate nationalism and slavery, protect African-American citizenship and supported industrial expansionism during the Gilded Age. Grant's attempt to be elected for a third term was unsuccessful.

THE STORY BEHIND GRANT'S *PERSONAL MEMOIRS*

What makes *Personal Memoirs* unique is how it got to be written and who the publisher was. The Century Company, publisher of a popular magazine noted for its maps and illustrations, was interested in Grant's life story. *Century Magazine's* editors were trying to convince Grant to write his memoirs in a series of articles for their magazine and to group the articles into a book. The magazine's executives wanted a story that would examine the Civil War from the general's perspective. They were even willing to pay

Grant an advance, something that was not regularly done at that time. Richard Watson Gilder submitted a proposal to Grant, who replied: "Do you really think that anyone would be interested in a book by me?"[8]

The Century Company continued to pursue Grant, offering him a 10 % royalty, a sizable sum for that time, and agreed to hire a staff of representatives to sell the book throughout the United States. They believed that they would be able to promote the work to the readers of their magazine and would be able to sell an initial printing of 25,000 copies. After negotiations with the Century Company, Grant's project ultimately was published by an unlikely hero, Mark Twain. He had obtained knowledge of Century's proposal and figured that he could outbid them. Twain was quite persuasive and flattering of Grant and his work and offered him more money. While Grant felt beholden to Century since they came to him first, he eventually was convinced that Twain should be the publisher. Grant accepted Twain's better offer, which proposed a $10,000 advance and a 75 % royalty. Finally, on February 27, 1885, Grant officially signed a publishing agreement with Charles Webster's company, and Twain delivered a much-needed initial check of $1000 to the ailing former president.

The project took a sharp turn in the fall of 1884, when Grant was diagnosed with cancer, which ultimately would prove fatal. By mid-April 1885, "Grant had finally completed all of the articles he had promised the Century (on Shiloh, Vicksburg, Chattanooga, and the Wilderness) and was plunging ahead in the race to complete his memoirs before the deterioration in his health made this impossible."[9] His penmanship had begun to deteriorate, making it difficult for others to read his manuscript. In the late stages of the writing, Grant had to dictate his thoughts.

Despite suffering from debilitating throat cancer, Grant worked diligently on his memoirs at his home in New York City and then from a cottage on the slopes of Mount McGregor in upstate New York, finishing only days before he died. Former staff officer Adam Badeau was hired to help research, locate relevant maps, fact check, and edit his work. He corrected the president's spelling and grammar. Badeau had been a part of Grant's military staff since 1864. Grant promised to pay him $5000 from the first $20,000 in royalties and an additional $5000 from the next $10,000.[10] A dispute arose, concerning not only the payment to Badeau but how he would be credited in *Personal Memoirs*. Grant subsequently fired him. Additionally, Badeau had published his own *Military History of Ulysses S. Grant* in 1881 and felt that Grant's book would be in direct competition with his. There were those who believed that Badeau was the real author of *Memoirs.* In the spring of 1886, an article in *The New York World* newspaper alleged that Grant was not the author of his memoirs. Colonel George Ihrie, who had served with him during the Mexican War, made the allegation. Ihrie believed that the book was actually written by Badeau with material provided by Grant. Other skeptics insinuated that Mark Twain was the true author of Grant's work. Grant vehemently denied the charge. Grant's memoir concludes with the Civil War and does not cover the post-war years; nor does it include his presidency, or his well-documented trip around the world.

Grant succumbed to his cancer on July 23, 1885. The book, *Personal Memoirs of Ulysses S. Grant,* went on to become both a critical and commercial success. (Fr. Barnes and Noble).[11] There are those who believed that by taking on the project of writing his memoirs, Grant may have helped to extend his life long enough to finish his manuscript. "Only a few minor shifts in Grant's daily routine marked the passage of the General's disease: Where before his writing had been strong, the letters of his words etched deeply in the unlined pages of his papers, now the letters were usually sloped, the penmanship was erring, the pages lined in order to set out markers for Grant's failing eyes."[12] During his final days, Grant found himself somewhat prophetic. "I feel that we are on the eve of a new era, when there is to be great harmony between the Federal and Confederate. I cannot stay to be a living witness to the correctness of the prophecy, but I feel it within me that it is to be so."[13]

The first edition of *Personal Memoirs of Ulysses S. Grant* was published by Charles L. Webster (Twain's nephew) in 1885. The original press run was sold by subscription. Customers could choose the book's binding with the two-volume deluxe leather edition selling for $100. More than 30,000 sets of the first edition were sold. Union Army veterans delivered the books and were given a 37-page manual titled "How to Introduce the *Personal Memoirs of Ulysses S. Grant*" to prepare for the delivery project. Twain had told Webster that he believed they could sell 300,000 of the two-volume sets, a goal they eventually reached. He instructed Webster to put together the best subscription department possible, complete with public relations.[14]

On February 27, 1886, Twain presented Julia Grant (the President's widow), with a check for $200,000, at that time the largest royalty payment in American publishing history. Over the next ten years, Julia Grant received almost $450,000 in royalties from the sale of *Personal Memoirs of Ulysses S. Grant*. (Perry p.233). "No previous book had sold so many copies in such a short period of time."[15]

Twain's publishing firm enjoyed an appreciable profit from the sale of Grant's memoirs even after he added up the cost of publicity and printing. Twain was overjoyed, but he soon learned that his firm was deeply in debt and within a few years was struggling."[16]

THE RELATIONSHIP BETWEEN ULYSSES S. GRANT AND MARK TWAIN (SAMUEL CLEMENS)

How did the unlikely friendship between Ulysses S. Grant and Mark Twain develop?

In 1883 Grant was encouraged to participate in an investment by a Wall Streeter named Ferdinand Ward. The investment turned out to be what can be best described as a Ponzi scheme. Grant ended up losing $100,000 of his own money plus an additional $150,000 he had borrowed from William Henry Vanderbilt. Since he was nearly broke, Grant chose to write his memoirs with the hope that he could leave sufficient funds for his wife and children to live on when he was gone. Twain helped rescue the ailing president both financially and socially and believed that encouraging Grant to complete the project extended his life. According to West Point English professor, Dr. Elizabeth Samet, "I think Twain admired Grant's persona and writing style, different as it was from so many of his more florid contemporaries."

"Grant never commented in writing on his relationships with Twain, but his family and friends did—in numerous letters and reminiscences. Twain himself was the friendship's key and chronicler."[17] "Twain now considered Ulysses S. Grant not simply a great soldier and former President, but also a good friend. Some of the most relaxing days he spent in New York away from his work had been with Grant."[18]

THE REVIEWS ARE IN

Of all the books written by presidents, Grant's one book, his *Personal Memoirs*, received a great deal of attention, both from the general public and from the academic community. It is still read and researched today. Revised and annotated editions have been periodically published by professors and historical researchers who have been able to provide additional, more current research, as well as alternative views of this important work.

Mark Twain wrote: "I had been comparing the memoirs with Caesar's Commentaries... I was able to say in all sincerity, that the same high merits distinguished both books—clarity of statement, directness, simplicity, unpretentiousness, manifest truthfulness, fairness and justice toward friend and foe alike, soldierly candor and frankness and soldierly avoidance of flowery speech. I placed the two books side by side upon the same high level, and I still think that they belonged there."[19]He believed that this work was one of the best memoirs ever written by a general. But then again, Twain was the publisher.

Even into the twenty-first century, *Personal Memoirs* continues to garner accolades. Grant's work has been listed in *The Officer's Professional Reading Guide Top 100.* The history department of the United States Military Academy publishes this guide. *Memoirs* was also selected as one of the top five books written by a US president by Washington Post author and journalist Walter R. Borneman. (June 26, 2014)

Other reviews were just as flattering. "The best book written by a US President was *Personal Memoirs of U.S. Grant*. The two volumes focus on Grant's time during the Civil War rather than his time as President."[20]

In 2017 an annotated edition—*The Personal Memoirs of Ulysses S. Grant, The Complete Annotated Edition*—was published. The editors of the Ulysses S. Grant Association's Presidential Library compiled this annotation. The chief editor of this project was Dr. John Marszalek, professor of history, Mississippi State University, who worked along with David S. Nolan and Louie P Gallo. Marszalek is the W.L. Giles Distinguished Professor of History Emeritus and managing editor of the Ulysses S. Grant Association. Marszalek noted that he was surprised by Grant's ability as a storyteller.

In 2019, Dr. Elizabeth Samet, Professor of English at the United States Military Academy at West Point, published a newer annotated edition. Samet had the benefit of having access to archives at the academy and was able to include additional maps and charts in this most recent edition. She also included her personal photographs of Grant's Tomb in New York and the Grant Memorial in Washington, D.C. Professor Samet said: "The one time in his life Grant did not maintain his silence was in his *Personal Memoirs*, and in its pages one can discover his cultivation of the coolness, common sense, and concentration that made victory possible."[21]

Bestselling and award-winning author and historian Ron Chernow had this to say about Grant's book. "*The Personal Memoirs of U.S Grant,* widely viewed as a masterpiece, is probably the foremost military memoir in the English language, written in a clear, simple style that transcends the torment of its composition."[22]

R. Manning Ancell is a former naval lieutenant commander and author who wrote the book *The Leader's Bookshelf* in 2017. He interviewed former Secretary of Defense James Mattis about books that he thought important for tactical and strategic leaders. Mattis observed: "You can't go wrong when you read Grant's *Memoirs*."[23]

The everyday citizens who purchased and read Grant's book were to be the ultimate arbiters of its value and success. The American people received a great deal more than a mere history book or autobiography from Grant. For millions of readers, his final words came to symbolize the lessons of a conflict that divided our nation and cost more than half a million lives. "Let us have peace," Grant wrote. (*Memoirs* ch. 67) It was his final goodbye to America. The dedication to *Personal Memoirs* reads: "These volumes are dedicated to the American Soldier and Sailor." He was a soldier's soldier to the end of his life.

(Library of Congress Prints and Photographic Division, LC-USZ62-13034)

Dwight David Eisenhower
Born: October 14, 1890- Denison, Texas
Died: March 28, 1969- Washington, D.C.
34th President- 1953-1961
Wife: Mamie Doud
Political Party- Republican
Undergraduate College: United States Military Academy (West Point)
(Buzzfeed art.)

"Leadership is the art of getting someone else to do something you want done because he wants to do it."

-Dwight D. Eisenhower

If I were to compare the lives and works of Grant and Eisenhower, this much can be said: One helped preserve the Union and the other helped save the world. Their preparation at West Point as leaders, military strategists, and thinkers helped pave the way for their successes on the battlefield and their abilities in the White House. Neither Grant nor Eisenhower had any previous political experience at the time they entered the Oval Office.

Eisenhower is recognized as one of the true heroes of World War II and, arguably, the single most important military figure of the war. He was the Allied commander who planned and led the Normandy Invasion on D-Day and the retaking of Europe from the Nazi stronghold. After the war, Eisenhower was appointed the first Supreme Commander of NATO forces and in 1953 was selected to be the president of Columbia University.

His prowess as a politician and president is quite often underestimated. Princeton University emeritus professor Fred Greenstein observed: "He (Eisenhower) was once assumed to have been a well-intentioned political innocent, but he emerges from the historical record as a self-consciously oblique political sophisticate with a highly distinctive leadership style." [24] In some circles Eisenhower is regarded as the "Hidden Hand President." Like his fellow West Point graduate, Ulysses S. Grant, Eisenhower utilized his organizational and leadership skills to serve as a two-term president.

CRUSADE IN EUROPE (1948)

Eisenhower's first book, *Crusade in Europe*, takes an in-depth look at his World War II career, his working closely with our British allies, and the planning of D-Day. He provides readers with a front-row seat with great detail, maps, lists of troop strengths, armaments, and analyses of the war from his vantage point as a general. He is meticulous in his description of the details for Operation Overlord and the Normandy Invasion. Eisenhower only briefly writes about the war in Pacific and the impact that it had on his efforts in the European theatre of operations.

This book, written only three years after the war ended, shows Eisenhower not as a braggart, but a leader and a diplomat, providing his readers with a narrative of the events of the war in Europe. It is also a cautionary tale, reminding us to be diligent and prepared for whatever future evils might come our way. Eisenhower goes into much detail about his relationship with General George Patton, including disagreements they had, and trying to juxtapose Patton's outstanding military mind with his personality and relationship with the press.

If the reader were looking for an encyclopedia-like account of World War II, *Crusade in Europe* would not be it. It is, however, well suited for a general readership and is often regarded as the single most complete story of the war.

The question is often asked: Did Eisenhower have any thoughts about what was going to happen to a postwar Germany? He commented in the book: "The future division of Germany did not influence our military plans for the final conquest of the country. Military plans, I believe, should be devised with the simple aim of speeding victory. I decided, however, that Berlin was not the logical or the most desirable objective for the forces of the western Allies."[25]

Those with an eye for historical precedent will note that at the Nazi surrender to the Allies, Ike followed a protocol similar to one used by Grant at Lee's surrender at Appomattox Court House: No fanfare; no terms but unconditional surrender.

Ike addressed issues other than military strategy in *Crusade in Europe*. The excerpt below focuses on an issue that has too often been overlooked when discussing World War II— race.

> "Prior to my arrival in England, censorship had been established by American headquarters on stories involving minor difficulties between Negro troops and other soldiers, or civilians. These incidents frequently involved social contacts between our Negro soldiers and British girls. The British population except in large cities and among wealthy classes lacks the racial consciousness that is so strong in the United States. The small-town British girl would go to a movie or dance with a Negro quite as readily as she would with anyone else, a practice that our white soldiers could not understand. Brawls often resulted, and our white soldiers were further bewildered when they found that the British press took a firm stand on the side of the Negro."[26]

In one of many political ironies, in 1957, President Eisenhower had to nationalize the Arkansas National Guard and send in troops from the 101st Airborne Division to quell a riot and allow nine African-American students to enroll in Little Rock Central High School.

Eisenhower worked very diligently on his book, and his style was a simple one. He worked with two editors on this project: Kenneth McCormick, editor-in-chief at Doubleday, and Joseph Barnes, foreign editor of the *New York Herald Tribune*. At the time of *Crusade in Europe*'s publication, Ike had not yet considered running for any public office, let alone the presidency of the United States. This book was simply Ike recounting his story of World War II without the pretense of using the book as a tool for political ambition, as other presidential candidates had done.

Crusade in Europe was so popular that in 1948, Twentieth Century Fox obtained the rights to Eisenhower's book and went on to produce the first in-depth documentary series specifically developed for television. This documentary, part of "The March of Time" series, aired on the ABC network. The television program included actual World War II film footage. The 26 weekly episodes earned both a Peabody Award and a Prime-Time Emmy for best public service, cultural or educational program.

REVIEW OF *CRUSADE IN EUROPE*

Eisenhower's first literary work was well received and highly regarded. The original first edition, published by Doubleday, was limited to 1426 copies, each of them signed by Eisenhower. "This stands head and shoulders above the other records of fighting men, in its simplicity, clarity, and the illumination it throws on the basic human relations of the men at the top. In his *Normandy to the Baltic,* Field Marshall Bernard Montgomery wrote: "We are still too close to the events to attempt a critical analysis of the campaign."

According to the Kirkus review of the book, readers get an objective view of the Allied military effort and cooperation to achieve total victory over the Axis powers. Eisenhower details the excruciating life and death decision-making in preparing for the Normandy assault. "It is a tribute to the men who fought on various fronts under the most trying conditions. It is a picture of the destruction and horror of war."[27]

MANDATE FOR CHANGE, 1953-1956: THE WHITE HOUSE YEARS (1963)

Eisenhower would not write another book until after his presidency ended. In the latter stages of the Second World War, Eisenhower was already being mentioned as a potential presidential candidate. At that time, he emphatically stated that he was not interested in a career in politics. Ike was the reluctant candidate. The hierarchy of the Republican Party finally wore Ike down and he relented. He said that he would run if nominated but would not actively seek the presidential nomination. Eisenhower was nominated at the 1952 Republican National Convention held in Chicago, following in the footsteps of other generals who went on to become President of the United States.

Mandate for Change was essentially a political autobiography. Eisenhower compares the euphoria of his victory on Election Night 1952 with May 8, 1945, the day when the Nazi war machine capitulated and surrendered, effectively ending World War II in Europe.

There were a number of critical issues facing his administration, both foreign and domestic. They included dealing with the changing role of NATO, resolving the stalemate in Korea and ending that war, dealing with the Suez crisis and a rising situation in Iran. Regarding Iran, Eisenhower wrote: "Another troubled area that compelled our concern during 1953 was Iran, a country of 19 million people, which shares a border with the Soviet Union and which holds beneath its soil a large percentage of the world's reserves of oil."[28] There was also a growing concern about an increasing US involvement in French Indo-China (Vietnam).

Domestically, Eisenhower worked through issues such as the Tennessee Valley Authority (TVA), farm surpluses, and the end of McCarthyism. He agonized whether to grant executive clemency to Ethel and Julius Rosenberg, who had been convicted of espionage and sentenced to death in 1951. Eisenhower stated: "The nature of the crime for which they have been found guilty as sentenced far exceeds that of the taking of the life of another citizen; it involves the deliberate betrayal of the entire nation."

Eisenhower was even mindful of the nuclear arms race and the role of atomic energy. He said: "...The United States pledges before you—and therefore before the world—its determination to help solve the fearful atomic dilemma—to devote its entire heart and mind to find the way by which the miraculous inventiveness of man shall not be dedicated to his death, but consecrated to his life." (Atoms for Peace" speech before the UN, December 8, 1953).[29] *Mandate for Change* p.105.

AT EASE: STORIES I TELL TO FRIENDS (1967)

Eisenhower's last book, *At Ease: Stories I Tell to Friends,* was published by Doubleday in 1967. This work is a folksy, low-key retrospective. He recalls stories of his days at the United States Military Academy at West Point. The book is peppered with military stories and tales of the war years, as one would expect. Ike also writes about his wife Mamie, and how difficult it was for her to be away from him for long periods of time.

A little-known fact about Dwight Eisenhower was that he was a more avid reader than the general public was led to believe. "His own library had over a thousand volumes, including *A History of Western Art* by John Ives Sewall, Bruce Catton's *Mr. Lincoln's Army* and *A Stillness at Appomattox*, multiple copies of the Bible, and of course, a selection of Western novels."[30]

Sadly, we have only three books written by so prominent a figure in the twentieth century. It will be up to the historians and scholars to fill in the blanks to complete the saga of America's last West Point President.

Note: "Thanks to (President) Truman's personal intervention, the IRS judged Eisenhower to be a nonprofessional writer and so taxed his income from this war memoir *Crusade in Europe* at the 25-percent capital gains rate rather than the 75-percent income tax rate."[31]

---

[1] Ulysses S. Grant. *Personal Memoirs* (Caleb Carr, editor) (New York: Modern Library, 1999), 15.

[2] Elizabeth Samet, ed. *Annotated Memoirs of Ulysses S. Grant* (New York: Liveright Publishing Corp., 2019), 43.

[3] Grant, p. xix.

[4] *Ibid.*, p. 18

[5] Grant, p. 117.

---

[6] *Ibid.*, p. 303.
[7] *Ib*id., p. 366.
[8] Mark Perry. *Grant and Twain:The Story of a Friendship that Changed America*
(New York: Random House, 2004), 63.
[9] Ibid., p. 194.
[10] Ron Chernow. *Grant.* (New York: Penguin Random House, 2017), 233.
[11] Samet, p. 31
[12] Perry, p. 195.
[13] Samet, (in Grant) p. 934.
[14] *Ibid.*, p. 141.
[15] Chernow, p. 953.
[16] Perry, pp. 233-34.
[17] *Ibid.*, p. 241.
[18] *Ibid.*, p. 140
[19] Mark Twain. *The Autobiography of Mark Twain.* Vol. II
(New York: Harper and Brothers, 1927)
[20] Kelsey Mulvey- Insider Picks in *Business Insider*, October 18, 2016 (accessed October 19, 2018.
[21] Samet, ed. p. xxiii.
[22] Chernow, p. 952.
[23] (From article by Amanda Macias, CNBC, published September 15, 2018
"The Extraordinary Reading Habits of Defense Secretary James Mattis" accessed September 1, 2019

[24] Fred Greenstein. *The Presidential Difference: Leadership Style From FDR to Clinton.* (New York: The Free Press, 2000), 191.
[25] Michael Korda. *Ike.* (New York: HarperCollins, 2007), 396.
[26] Dwight D. Eisenhower. *Crusade in Europe*
(New York: Doubleday and Company. 1948), 58-59.
[27] Kirkus Review: *Crusade in Europe*. Accessed October 21, 2019.
[28] *Ibid.*, p. 159.
[29] *Mandate for Change*, p. 105.
[30] Tevi Trop. *What Jefferson Read, Ike Watched, and Obama Tweeted*
(Washington, D.C.: Regnery Publishing, Inc., 2013), 184.

[31] Nancy Gibbs and Michael Duffy. *The Presidents Club- Inside the World's Most Exclusive Fraternity*. (New York: Simon & Schuster, 2012), 65.

CHAPTER FOUR
THE PROFESSOR PRESIDENT

(Library of Congress Prints and Photographic Division, LOC dig-det-4a26353)

Woodrow Wilson
Born: December 28, 1856- Staunton, Virginia
Died: March 4, 1924- Washington, DC
28th President of the United States
Term: 1913-1921
Wives: Ellen Axson, Edith Galt
Political Party: Democrat
Undergraduate College: Princeton University (Then called the College of New Jersey)
Nobel Peace Prize Recipient- 1919

"Political liberty is the right of those who are governed to adjust government to their own needs and interests."[1]

With the election of Woodrow Wilson in 1912 as the twenty-eighth President of the United States, America got its first truly academic president. Educated at Princeton University in New Jersey, where he later taught and eventually became the university's president, Wilson produced numerous writings, mostly in the area of political science, that were scholarly in nature. While most previous presidents had attended college, and several earned law degrees, Woodrow Wilson was the first, and to this date, the only president to have an earned Ph.D. He taught at the college level, and went on to become president of a prestigious Ivy League university, Princeton. He was also elected Governor of New Jersey in 1910, a victory that launched his political career.

As a student and a professor, Wilson produced quite a bit of writing, and his works were generally well received, especially in history and political science circles. He spent a total of twenty-five years on Princeton's campus, first as a student, then as a professor, and lastly, as its president. These experiences foreshadowed some of the personality traits that were later to manifest themselves in his presidency. They were also reflected in his writings.

CONGRESSIONAL GOVERNMENT (ORIGINALLY PUBLISHED BY RIVERSIDE PRESS-HOUGHTON MIFFLIN CO., 1885)

Finding so much of his studies distasteful and pointless, Wilson typically poured his energies into an independent writing project, compiling the ideas of his old senior essay from Princeton into a book, the most important he would ever write. Published in 1885 during his second year of graduate school, *Congressional Government* was modeled closely on the writing of his English hero, Walter Bagehot, (journalist, political analyst and editor of *The Economist*.) It called for an introduction of British parliamentary methods so that strong leaders would again emerge to guide America, as could never happen with the current congressional committees.

"Wilson's greatest satisfaction came in writing *Congressional Government*, a book that grew out of a series of unpublished essays."[2] The first half of the book was written during the winter of 1884. It included an introduction and two essays on the US House of Representatives and how the United States Congress operates. He felt that the legislative branch exerted too much power and dominated the government. He further believed that the power of the president had been on the wane since Abraham Lincoln. Wilson cited the presidencies from Andrew Johnson to Ulysses S. Grant, James Garfield and Chester Arthur. He wrote: "I want to contribute to our literature what no American has ever contributed—studies in the philosophy of institutions."[3] His thesis was that the governmental system of the United States should more clearly mirror the British parliamentary system. The book, 333 pages in length, with a gilded blue cover, signaled Wilson's arrival as a rising star in the arena of political science and thought.

Johns Hopkins University determined that the work satisfied its dissertation requirements and awarded him a Ph.D. *Congressional Government* sold 1,000 copies in its initial press run and continued to be published in small quantities for the next fifteen years. "Wilson's name became widely known, but at nearly thirty he was still no important person shaping men's destinies."[4]

REVIEWS OF *CONGRESSIONAL GOVERNMENT*

The reviews for the work were mixed, but the *Minneapolis Daily Tribune* called the book "the best critical writing on the American Constitution, which has appeared since the Federalist Papers."[5] A review by Gamiel Bradford, in *The Nation*, February 12, 1885, called the volume "one of the most important books dealing with political subjects, which have ever issued from the American Press."[6]

In the final analysis, *Congressional Government* was believed to be Wilson's most noteworthy book. He wrote: "We are the first Americans to hear our own countrymen ask whether the Constitution is still adapted to serve the purposes for which it was intended: the first to entertain any serious doubts about the superiority of our own institutions as compared with the systems of Europe: the first to think of remodeling the administrative machinery of the federal government and of finding new forms of responsibility upon congress."[7] Wilson went on to write: "It is at once curious and instructive to note how we have been forced into practically amending the Constitution without constitutionally amending it."

DIVISION AND REUNION (1893)

Wilson' s next work received much less attention than the others. *Division and Reunion* was the third installment of the Epochs in American History series and is an historical account of the history of the United States between 1829 and 1889. The book is divided into five parts and begins with the inauguration of President Andrew Jackson and concludes with a discussion of the great wealth-building in America.[8]

Longmans, Green and Company in New York first published *Division and Reunion* in 1893. The 351-page work included five maps, a suggested reading list and a suggested education guide for readers and teachers. The other books in the Epoch Series were *The Colonies, 1492-1750* by Reuben Gold Thwaites, and *Formation of the Union 1750-1829* by Albert Bushnell Hart. Hart, a professor of history at Harvard University, was the general editor of the entire series.

HISTORY OF THE AMERICAN PEOPLE (1902)

Wilson's seminal, most detailed work was the five-volume *History of the American People.* Harper and Brothers, a publisher who seems to like books written by men who would become president, published this set in 1902. This set of books is heavily illustrated with maps, charts, book passages and drawings. "The imposing five-volume set made him [Wilson] one of the best-known historians in the country."[9]

Volume One begins with the founding of the Virginia Company. "When the history of English settlement in America begins… The Elizabethan Age is over and the sober, contentious seventeenth century has come with its perplexed politics, its schismatic creeds, its scheming rivalries in trade."[10]

Volume Five is devoted to Reunion and Nationalization. It delves into the reunification of the nation after the Civil War and Wilson's thoughts about the Reconstruction effort.

"… It seemed mere weakness to accord the Southern States their old place in the Union without exacting of them something more than mere submission. Should their social system be left untouched, their old life and power given back to them to be used as before…"[11]

Many agree that this was not Wilson's best literary effort and was primarily written for monetary gain. Other critics view the work as having cultural importance and part of the general fund of knowledge base for our society. During a visit to the White House by King Albert of Belgium, President Wilson gave him a specially bound set of the books, personally autographed.

CONSTITUTIONAL GOVERNMENT OF THE UNITED STATES (1908)

Wilson wrote a follow-up book to *Congressional Government*. He titled it *Constitutional Government in the United States* and published it in 1908. This book is essentially a series of lectures that Wilson delivered at Columbia University in 1907. The lectures offer a re-examination of a number of his previous works. Wilson asserts that the Constitution of the United States is an evolutionary document that has changed over the years to meet the needs of an ever-changing country.[12]

In *Constitutional Government*, Woodrow Wilson first provides his readers with a detailed historical background of the Magna Carta (1215) and the effect it would have on future democracies. He then goes on to address each of the three branches of the United States federal government: the executive, legislative and judicial. Wilson then addresses the issue of the relationships between the individual states and the federal government, also highlighting the differences between the states themselves, using the institution of slavery as an example. This book, as well as *Congressional Government*, was written without the benefit of Wilson having sat in the chair in the Oval Office. Some of his ideologies would change as he approached the presidency—first as an academic and then ultimately as a politician.

THE NEW FREEDOM (1913)

In 1913, now in the White House, Wilson published *The New Freedom: A Call for the Emancipation of the Generous Energies of a People.* He was quite candid in his introduction. "I have not written a book since the (Presidential) campaign. I did not write the book at all. It is the result of the editorial literary skill of Mr. William Bayard Hale, who has put together here in the right sequences the more suggestive portions of my campaign speeches."[13]

Within this work, Wilson railed against big business and their disproportionate influence in the federal government. He observed: "Every time it has come to a question, these gentlemen have been yielded to and their demands have been treated as the demands that should be followed as a matter of course."[14] In *The New Freedom*, Wilson goes on to question the role of the common people in the federal government. "The government of the United States is a foster child of the special interest. The noble charter of fundamental laws given us by the convention of 1787 is still our constitution, but it is now our form of government rather in name than in reality, the form of the constitution being one of careful, ideal balances whilst the actual form of our present government is simply a scheme of congressional supremacy."[15]

Should we have expected more from a professor turned president and what might have been? Perhaps if Wilson had remained at Princeton he would have been a more prolific author. As President of the United States, Wilson had to deal with America's entry into World War I, promoting his Fourteen Points, and his passion for establishing the League of Nations. Then on October 2, 1919, Wilson suffered a debilitating stroke that left him partially paralyzed and blind in one eye. For a while he was unable to speak or move. A promising post-presidential literary career came to a sudden and unexpected end.

Wilson had periodically been working on another possible book project, which he tentatively titled *Philosophy of Politics*. This work, however, was never published.

---

[1] Woodrow Wilson. *Constitutional Government of the United States* (New York: Columbia University Press, 1964), 4 (originally published in1911)
[2] A. Scott Berg. *Wilson*. (New York: G.P. Putnam's Sons, 2013), 95.
[3] *Ibid.*

[4] W. Barksdale Maynard. *Woodrow Wilson: Princeton to the Presidency.*
(New Haven: Yale University Press, 2008), 29-30.
[5] Berg. p. 100

[6] The Papers of Woodrow Wilson- Project Records MC-178 (Mudd Library, Princeton University)
[7] Woodrow Wilson. *Congressional Government: A Study in American Politics*
(Cambridge, Massachusetts: The Riverside Press, 1901), 4.
[8] Berg, p. 121.
[9] Berg, p. 134.
[10] Woodrow Wilson. *A History of the American People* (Five Volumes)
(New York: Harper and Brothers Publishers,1901), Vol. I. p. 1.
[11] Wilson. Vol. V. p. 4)
[12] Chapter five manuscript-Courtesy of Mudd Library, Princeton University.
[13] Woodrow Wilson. *The New Freedom: A Call for the Emancipation of the Generous Energies of a People* (New York: Doubleday, Page and Company, 1913), vi.
[14] *Ibid.*, p. 58
[15] Wilson. Chapter 1. p. 5

CHAPTER FIVE
MISUNDERSTOOD PRESIDENTS

(Library of Congress Prints and Photographs Division- LC-Dig-NPCC-03577)

Herbert Hoover
Born- August 10, 1874- West Branch, Iowa
Died- October 20, 1964- New York City, New York
31st President
Term: 1929-1933
Wife: Lou Henry
Party: Republican
Undergraduate College- Stanford University

"There are some principles that cannot be compromised. Either we shall have a society based upon ordered liberty and the initiative of the individual, or we shall have a planned society that means dictation no matter what you call it or who does it. There is no halfway ground. They cannot be mixed."

— Herbert Hoover

Herbert Hoover may be one of America's most misunderstood and unloved presidents. His name continues to show up on lists as one of America's worst chief executives. He was educated at Stanford University (one of its first graduates) with a degree in mining engineering and had a distinguished career in public service prior to being elected president. During World War I, he headed the Commission for Relief in Belgium and received many accolades for his efforts. Hoover also served the Wilson administration in the American Relief Administration (ARA) and the US Food Administration.

In the fall of 1919, Hoover returned to the United States, having been sent to Europe at the request of President Woodrow Wilson, deeply moved and concerned about the plight of the people. They were starving, they were ill, many facing death. His efforts on behalf of the American Relief Administration made him a humanitarian hero on the Continent. He had seen the ravages of socialism and the "Great War," and began to formulate the thesis for his first book *American Individualism.*

AMERICAN INDIVIDUALISM (1922)

American Individualism was published in 1922 while Hoover was serving as Secretary of Commerce. He believed that individuals are the root of American greatness, not the government or its institutions. Hoover wrote about the beliefs and values that make America unique. He felt that Americans could continue the nation's progress if we could preserve our individualism. His writing echoed his conservative American ideology. "Individualism has been the primary force of American civilization for three centuries. It is our sort of individualism that supplied the motivations of America's political, economic and spiritual institutions in all these years."[1]

Hoover was offered the opportunity to publish two articles based on the book in *American Magazine* for $25,000. Instead, he chose to have them published in the *Saturday Evening Post* for $10,000.[2] (George H. Nash, Introduction to American Individualism, pp.15-16)

American Individualism was subsequently published in Russian in 1924 and in Polish in 1930. Hoover's distaste for war lingered long after his presidency. "Older men declare war. But it is youth that must fight and die. And it is youth who must inherit the tribulation, the sorrow, and the triumphs that are the aftermath of war." [3] (Speech given at Republican National Convention, 1944, Chicago, Illinois)

Hoover wrote numerous articles and other books championing his conservative political values. In his writings he warned about yielding too much power to the federal government. (History.com/topics/us-presidents/Herbert-hoover) accessed 12-18-18.

THE CHALLENGE TO LIBERTY (CHARLES SCRIBNER'S SONS. 1934)

Herbert Hoover had long been one of Franklin Roosevelt's arch-critics. He directed much of his post-presidential writings to make public his views on FDR and the New Deal.

The Challenge to Liberty is one of Hoover's best-known works and was written after his defeat by Franklin D. Roosevelt in the election of 1932. It was written during the Great Depression and before World War II.

Hoover warns his readers that the most fundamental principles of liberty were being challenged by Nazism, Fascism, communism, and socialism, as well as by FDR's New Deal. He felt that America was heading down the slippery slope to socialism. He was deeply concerned about individual states ceding too much authority to the federal government. Hoover singled out the National Recovery Act, the Agricultural Adjustment Act, and the Banking Act for his particular disdain. Portions of this book were published in the *Saturday Evening Post* in the September 8, 1934 issue. *The Challenge to Liberty* was also chosen as a Book-of-the-Month Club selection. The book was the best-selling non-fiction book in New York City with over 100,000 copies sold by March 1935.

However, not everyone was in agreement with what the former president wrote. FDR's Secretary of Interior Harold Ickes noted: "Mr. Hoover and those who think along with him don't seem to be concerned with the masses of people who want decent living conditions and jobs with fair wages." [4]

Still very much a public figure, Hoover traveled around the country reinforcing those principles and concerns he had written about.

"A whole people with the ballot in their hands possess the most conclusive and unlimited power ever entrusted to humanity. If that power is exercised rightly, then America will prosper morally, spiritually, and in its daily occupations. If it is exercised under the spell of hate or selfish purpose or under intimidation, it will drive this nation upon the rocks of destruction." [5] *(Speech given by Herbert Hoover, October 30, 1936, Denver, Colorado)*

"Our present difficulties, as great as they are, do not justify the assumption that a system of life builded (sic) on such sacrifice over a century and a half with such a record of achievement should be discarded or crippled, or that the philosophy of Liberty is all wrong, or even that we 'must sacrifice some of our liberties.'" [6]

In *Challenge to Liberty,* Hoover asserts his belief that the New Deal is taking away some of our inherent liberties that many in the country had fought for. He possessed rigid views about the New Deal. He objected to Roosevelt's closing of the banks and felt that FDR's policies were a threat to individual freedom. He also railed against the evils of bureaucracy as well as socialism. Hoover wrote: "Bureaucracy cannot replace the judgment of millions of individuals striving in their own interest. The government cannot compel energy and enterprise upon which productive power rests."[7]

Hoover laid out several of his philosophical views and thoughts about American democracy, challenging government bureaucracy and over-regulation. In reference to the spread of bureaucracy, Hoover warned: "Congress cannot run business but business can run Congress—to bankruptcy of Liberty."[8] He illustrates the effects of government spending if left unchecked, and how it can lead to massive budget deficits.

Hoover goes on to write about the uniqueness of American Liberalism, as differentiated from its European counterparts. "American Liberalism—it has always been living creed advancing to meet the problems of our particular world."[9] He believed that the American version of liberalism was a living and growing ideal.

Hoover challenged the existing administration to take action to prevent disasters. He notes: "We need revision and coordination of our state and federal regulatory laws in many other directions over railroads, electric power, and other semi-natural monopolies, over waste of our natural resources and over destructive competition with reduced child labor and stewardship."[10]

THE MEMOIRS OF HERBERT HOOVER (1951-1952)

Hoover wrote a three-volume memoir in 1951 and 1952. The first volume, *Years of Adventure,* encompassed the years 1874 to 1920. Volume two, *The Cabinet and the Presidency,* discusses the period between 1920 and 1933. The third and final volume, *The Great Depression*, covers the years 1929-1941. Hoover candidly wrote: "No matter how much emotion a President may feel at all these aberrations of the democratic process, he cannot, or at least should not, display it lest he injure the process itself."[11]

THE ORDEAL OF WOODROW WILSON (1958)

Hoover attended the Paris Peace Conference in 1919 and fully understood the parameters of the 14 Points and the impact of the Treaty of Versailles. His intuition and understanding of the treaty led him to believe that it would eventually lead to another war. In *The Ordeal of Woodrow Wilson*, Hoover writes of his support for Wilson and defends his actions at the conference. This was a rare literary event—the first book written by a president about another president—a Republican writing about a Democrat.

The editors of *American Heritage Magazine* wrote: "Hoover shared Wilson's ideals and aspirations and saw them, after endless man-killing struggles, dashed in large part to earth. Mr. Hoover writes not only with the grace born of simplicity, wide experience, and clear originality, but also humor and sympathy."[12]

It was not until 2014 when George W. Bush chose to write about his father that one president decided to pen a book about another president.

FISHING FOR FUN – AND TO WASH YOUR SOUL (1963)

Hoover did take some time from his more serious political writing to pen a lighthearted book about one of his favorite pastimes—fishing. This short 89-page book includes a number of pen and ink drawings by artist Bill Hoffman. The former president wrote about fish and fishermen as well as fishing lures and tackle.

FREEDOM BETRAYED (2011)

Hoover was writing and compiling material for a monumental book project at the time of his death in 1964. Edited by Hoover biographer and author, Dr. George H. Nash, this 957-page volume, with many footnotes, was published in 2011. As in several of his other writings, Hoover challenges and criticizes the foreign policies of Franklin Delano Roosevelt from the beginning of World War II and continuing through the development of the Cold War with the Soviet Union. He opens the door to the possibility of intrigue in the State Department during World War II. Hoover also believes that Roosevelt strived to appease Stalin. *Freedom Betrayed* provides the readers with a window through which to view American diplomacy through the mid-twentieth century. Hoover wrote: "I believe that throughout this period, the fate of mankind has been determined less by military action than by the decisions of political leaders."

THE CRUSADE YEARS, 1933-1955: HERBERT HOOVER'S LOST MEMOIRS ON THE NEW DEAL ERA AND ITS AFTERMATH (2013)

While he was researching the Hoover archives for *Freedom Betrayed,* Dr. Nash came across another unfinished manuscript that was to be titled *The Crusade Years*. This work was a memoir that Hoover had been working on in the 1940s and 1950s and never finished. With the permission of the Hoover family foundation and the Hoover Institution, Nash pieced together material that historians and scholars were unaware of.

According to Nash's analysis of Hoover's writings, the former president was still at odds with the New Deal. He wrote of the "crusade against collectivism" and the need to rescue the nation from FDR. Hoover also wrote about the Presidential election of 1940 and his desire to get back into politics.

In this memoir, Hoover also wanted to be remembered for his philanthropic work, dating back to the Belgian relief effort after World War I. The Crusade Years highlighted his work with the Boys Clubs of America. Through it all, Hoover wanted to remind his readers of the importance of perseverance in the face of adversity and keeping the faith.[13]

Hoover became friends with another misunderstood chief

executive. Over the years, he developed a cordial relationship with Richard Nixon. They dined together several times a year, discussing current political and foreign policy issues. Nixon valued Hoover's opinion. Richard Nixon had this to say about Hoover in his book *Leaders:* "Few leaders live to hear the verdict (of history). Herbert Hoover was an exception.

No leader in American history was more viciously vilified. Deserted by his friends and maligned by his enemies, he finally triumphed over adversity. In the twilight of his life Hoover stood tall above his detractors. Hoover was articulate and a prolific writer, having penned about 15 books. He should probably be ranked in the top five of the presidential author list. His life illustrates de Gaulle's favorite line from Sophocles: "One must wait until evening to see how splendid the day has been." [14]

(Library of Congress Print and Photographic Division, LC-USZ62-13037)

Richard M. Nixon
Born- January 9,1913- Yorba Linda, California
Died- April 22,1994- New York City, New York
37th President
Term: 1969-1974
Wife: Thelma "Pat" Ryan
Party: Republican
Undergraduate College: Whittier College

"There has long been a widespread belief in the United States that what the country really needs is a top-flight businessman to run the government, someone who has proven that he can manage a large-scale enterprise efficiently and effectively. This misses the mark. Management is one thing. Leadership is another."[15] So writes Richard Nixon in the opening pages of his best-selling book, *Leaders*. Warren G. Bennis of the University of California's business school summed up Nixon's comment this way: "Managers have as their goal to do things right. Leaders have as their goal to do the right thing."[16]

Richard M. Nixon was the author of nine books, eight of which were best sellers and attracted widespread readers' attention. His first book, *Six Crises*, was published in 1962 (Doubleday and Company, 459 pp.) after serving two terms as Eisenhower's Vice President and after his bitter defeat by John F. Kennedy in the close 1960 presidential election. The suggestion to write was given to him by former First Lady Mamie Eisenhower.

Nixon had received a copy of *Profiles in Courage* personally from John Kennedy and decided to write a quasi-memoir in a similar style. Nixon's book examines his role in several major historical events that Nixon believed were seminal issues in his career at that time. They included his role in the trial of Alger Hiss, The "Checkers Speech," having to assume presidential duties upon Eisenhower's heart attack, having his motorcade attacked during a trip to Argentina, the "Kitchen Debate" with Soviet Premier Nikita Khrushchev in Moscow, and his 1960 presidential campaign. *Six Crises* sold over 300,000 copies. *Life Magazine* serialized several of his stories.

Charles Lichtenstein, a staff assistant during the Nixon administration, who also served as a United Nations diplomat during the Reagan administration, supposedly ghostwrote this book. *Washington Post* journalist and author Walter R. Borneman named *Six Crises* as one of the five best books written by a US president.[17] Notes, memoranda, and drafts related to the publication of *Six Crises* are presently located at the Richard Nixon Presidential Library in Yorba Linda, California. Access to these materials, administered by the National Archives and Records Administration (NARA), is currently restricted.

LEADERS (1982)

Leaders: Profiles and Reminiscences of Men Who Have Shaped the Modern World was published by Warner Books in 1982. *Leaders* examines six world leaders through Nixon's eyes, as he knew all them during the course of his political career. Those included were Winston Churchill, Charles De Gaulle, Douglas MacArthur, Konrad Adenauer, Nikita Khrushchev, and Zhou Enlai. These were men who, according to the author, changed the world. There are photo sections in this book and at least one photo of each of the leaders with Richard Nixon. Readers will find dozens of photos of the leaders analyzed, with Nixon posing in his various roles as Vice President and President. Nixon noted: "This book is a product of study and experience stretching over the better part of a lifetime. What I have learned about leaders and leadership has come from a combination of reading, observation, the advice of expert practitioners, and the experience of doing it."[18]

NO MORE VIETNAMS (ARBOR HOUSE PUBLISHERS. 1985)

This best-selling book analyzes the American military involvement in Southeast Asia. It delves into the role of four US Presidents, and Congress, as well as the anti-war movement that was pervasive at the time, and the prominence of the media in reporting about the war to the American people. Nixon believed that the war was winnable. He illustrated that four presidents, the media, Congress and the anti-war movement all impacted the public view of the success /failure of the Vietnam War. He said: "Many who were seeing war for the first time were so shocked at what they saw that they said this war was immoral. What they really meant was that all war was terrible. They were right in saying peace was better than war. But they were wrong in failing to ask themselves whether what was immoral in Vietnam was substantially different from what happened in other wars." [19]

IN THE ARENA – A MEMOIR OF VICTORY, DEFEAT, AND RENEWAL (1990)

In what would be one of Nixon's last books, this gifted writer discusses in detail Watergate, his decision to resign the presidency, and his subsequent pardon by President Gerald Ford. Once again, as in *No More Vietnams*, Nixon offers his own critique of the press coverage in one of the seminal events of his presidency. In this memoir, Nixon still shows the desire to return to life in the public arena. In a sense, he fashions himself like Herbert Hoover—misunderstood, much maligned and underappreciated.

---

[1] Herbert Hoover. *American Individualism.*
(West Branch Iowa: Herbert Hoover Presidential Library Association, 1989), 58.
Original copyright 1922.

[2] George H. Nash, Introduction to *American Individualism*, pp.15-16

[3] Speech given at Republican National Convention, 1944, Chicago, Illinois.

[4] *The New York Times*, September 5, 1934. p. 15)

[5] *Speech given by Herbert Hoover, October 30, 1936, Denver, Colorado*

[6] Herbert Hoover, *The Challenge to Liberty*

(West Branch Iowa: Herbert Hoover Presidential Library Association, 1989), 102.
Original copyright 1934.
[7] *Ibid.*, p. 157.
[8] *Ibid.*, p. 161.
[9] *Ibid.*, p. 83.
[10] *Ibid.*, p. 189.
[11] Herbert Hoover. *The Memoirs of Herbert Hoover. Volume III-The Great Depression 1929-1941* (New York: MacMillian, 1951), 104.
[12] Editorial staff, *American Heritage Magazine*. June, 1958. Vol. 9, Issue 4.
(accessed January 7, 2020)
[13] *The University Bookman* interview with Dr. George H. Nash, February 16,2014.
[14] Richard Nixon. *Leaders: Profiles and Reminiscences of Men Who Have Shaped the Modern World.* (New York: Warner Books, 1982), 345.
[15] Richard Nixon. *Leaders: Profiles and Reminiscences of Men Who Have Shaped the Modern World.* (New York: Warner Books, 1982), 4.
[16] *Ibid.*
[17] "Five Best Books by American Presidents, *The Washington Post*, June 26, 2014)
[18] *Leaders*, p. 346,
[19] Richard Nixon. *No More Vietnams.* (New York: Arbor House, 1985). 16.

CHAPTER SIX
THE PREACHER PRESIDENT

(Library of Congress Photographic and Prints Division, LC-DIG-ppmsca-09769)

Jimmy Carter (James Earl Carter)
Born: October 1, 1924- Plains, Georgia
39th President
Term: 1977-1981
Wife: Eleanor Rosalynn Smith
Political Party: Democrat
Undergraduate College: United States Naval Academy
Nobel Peace Prize Recipient- 2002

"A nation's domestic and foreign policies should be derived from the same standards of ethics, honesty and morality which are characteristic of the individual citizens of the nation. The people of this nation are inherently unselfish, open, honest, decent, competent, and compassionate. Our government should be the same...."

-Jimmy Carter, *Why Not the Best?*

Jimmy Carter is the second most prolific president-author, having penned over two dozen books. Many political analysts believe that John F. Kennedy's *Profiles in Courage* was the first book to launch a presidential bid. Almost every candidate (and would-be candidate) since has written a book making public his or her vision for our country. If the candidate has enough public persona, he (or she) can get on practically every TV news and talk show, thus providing them with free media coverage, and if they are fortunate, make money. Carter was no different, using *Why Not the Best* as his "introduction" book. His idea for the title came about in an unusual way.

WHY NOT THE BEST (1975)

During Carter's initial interview in 1949 for a job with America's new nuclear submarine program, the young naval officer met with Admiral Hyman Rickover. He proudly told Rickover that he had finished in the top 10 percent of his Naval Academy class. Unimpressed Rickover asked: "Did you always do your best?" The young officer stammered and admitted he had not. "Why not?" Rickover asked, turning his back and ending the interview. Carter continued sitting on an uncomfortable chair that Rickover had prepared with the front legs two inches shorter than the back ones, and then stumbled out of the room, certain he had washed out. The admiral was known to use the odd chair as a tactic to throw candidates off and test them. Rickover brought Carter on board, however, and he always assumed it was because of his honesty. This seminal event became the impetus for the title of his presidential campaign book *Why Not the Best*? This was his first literary effort.[1] Admiral Rickover remained one of Carter's most admired individuals.

Why Not the Best? was used as a springboard to launch Carter's presidential bid. The bestseller eventually sold almost one million copies in hardback and paperback editions. The idea for the book came from Hamilton Jordan, who was one of Carter's campaign strategists. Carter, then the governor of Georgia, wrote this book by himself, with some editorial help from the associate editor of the *Atlanta Journal Constitution.* The book highlighted Carter's childhood, his military career, religious beliefs and relationship with his parents.

Carter's original publisher, Broadman Press, essentially an evangelical printer, rolled out *Why Not the Best*? on October 1, Carter's birthday. The release meshed nicely with the coming holiday shopping season and well in advance of the critical New Hampshire Primary, slated for February 24.

Years later, in 1996, a new edition of Carter's first book, *Why Not the Best?* was reprinted, now titled *Why Not the Best- The First Fifty Years*. Historian Douglas Brinkley, who wrote the introduction to the new edition noted, "Once Carter had won his party's nomination, the book became more of a memorable souvenir than required reading."[2]

Candidate Carter received no cash advance for his work but instead requested hardbound copies, which he autographed and distributed to supporters and members of the press. Additional copies were given to canvassers in New Hampshire, who distributed them door-to-door in the run up to the primary. Other copies were sold for five dollars each at campaign rallies.

In *Why Not the Best?* Carter noted that he believed his membership in the Trilateral Commission had given him a unique insight into dealing with both national as well as international leaders and a diverse array of subjects, especially on the topic of foreign affairs.[3] The Commission is a non-governmental forum that brings together experts from around the world in the fields of business, government and education.

Throughout Carter's life, his writings underwent a metamorphosis, beginning with the political, moving to the biographical and personal and most recently focusing on the evangelical and how personal faith became an integral part of his life.

TURNING POINT- A CANDIDATE, A STATE AND NATION COME OF AGE (1992)

In *Turning Point*, Carter paints a picture of life in rural Georgia after the Brown v. Board of Education Supreme Court decision. He is the outsider when it comes to segregation. Carter exposes in vivid detail his first run for political office as a Georgia state senator in 1962. He unveils the rampant corruption of the state Democratic Party and how his opponent stuffed ballot boxes and rigged the election. With the aid of an attorney and an investigative reporter, Carter goes about challenging the election results and proceeds to get the outcome reversed in his favor, thus launching his political career. He also provides a narrative about his refusal to join the local White Citizens Council, a schism that alienates him from his neighbors and former friends.

We also begin to see in this work Carter's rising interest in championing human rights, an issue that will become part of the fabric of the man, well after his presidency. *Turning Points* also contains an appendix where he describes the Atlanta Project, a program designed to help the urban poor.

AN HOUR BEFORE DAYLIGHT: MEMORIES OF A RURAL BOYHOOD (2001)

Carter's autobiography of his youth paints a vivid picture of the segregated society that existed in the rural South during the Great Depression. Carter writes about his father, a peanut farmer in rural Plains, Georgia, and how he struggled to make a living. He also shares stories of his mother, who was a nurse. The narrative covers Carter's boyhood years, including his friendships with several African-American boys, something that was taboo in rural Georgia at that time.

He writes about his going to church and how faith became such an important part of his life. The book concludes with Carter getting ready to leave Plains for the United States Naval Academy in Annapolis, Maryland. The former president writes: "My own life was shaped by a degree of personal intimacy between black and white people that is now almost completely unknown and largely forgotten."

An Hour Before Daylight: Memories of a Rural Boyhood, became a bestseller and was a runner up for the 2002 Pulitzer Prize for biography.

THE HORNET'S NEST (2004)

In 2004, Carter decided to move away from biography and politics and write a novel. He was the first president to write a full-length novel and was the only one to do so until Bill Clinton's joint effort with acclaimed novelist James Patterson in 2018. *The Hornet's Nest* is set in Colonial America. Carter developed his characters within the context of historical events taking place in the colonies while they were under British rule. (Note: Carter had already written fifteen books by the time *The Hornet's Nest* was published.) The book weaves in the role of the south, particularly in the Florida-Georgia area, from 1763-1783, in the battle for American independence. In this effort Carter reveals his commitment to historical accuracy within the framework of his characters. This, however, leads the plot to get bogged down in the history. His narrative also illustrates the plight of the Native Americans. The main characters get swept up in the revolt against the British.

The Hornet's Nest did not receive critical acclaim despite the fact that Carter did a significant amount of historical research for the book. One reviewer noted: "...you can, alas, have too much of a good thing, maybe 480 or so pages too much. We know Carter the submarine officer, nuclear engineer, peanut farmer, governor, commander-in-chief, Nobel peacemaker and global democracy monitor well enough, we may even have read some of his previous 16 books; the memoirs, histories, poems and children's stories. But a novel...this novel? For the truth is, that Carter has produced the worst of all offerings—an unreadable book."[4]

OUR ENDANGERED VALUES: AMERICA'S MORAL CRISIS (2005)

This book was listed as number one on *The New York Times* non-fiction bestseller list. Carter addresses a wide variety of issues. They include separation of church and state, women's rights, the death penalty, civil liberties, the environment, and homosexuality. Carter also asks the question: What is a superpower? He points to how partisan every issue has become in the political arena.

The book is an attempt to remake Carter's legacy and the topics addressed will appear in some of his subsequent works. *Our Endangered Values* was one of two Carter books that earned a Grammy Award for Best Spoken Word album. The other of Carter's books to earn that distinction was *A Full Life: Reflections at Ninety*.

The former president is a very religious man and still teaches Sunday school at the Maranatha Baptist Church in Plains, Georgia. It is not surprising, knowing Carter's background, that his more recent writings are about topics of faith. Carter hopes that his abiding faith and the work of the Carter Center will be his legacy

PALESTINE: PEACE NOT APARTHEID (2006)

With the publication of *Palestine: Peace Not Apartheid*, Carter's writing moves back into the political arena, this time in the hotbed of the Middle East. He caused a great deal of controversy and created more than a few enemies with the publication of this book. While Carter was still hopeful for a peaceful solution to the Israel-Palestine conflict, he squarely laid the blame for the lack of progress on the obstinacy and the unrealistic (according to Carter) demands of the government of Israel. He does meticulously lay out the troubled history of the conflict that is helpful if you have not been paying attention to the situation in the Middle East. Carter uses his cachet as broker of the 1978 Camp David Accords and recipient of the Nobel Peace Prize in 2002 to make his case for a peaceful two-state solution. Carter is less critical of Yasser Arafat and Mahmoud Abbas than he is of Israel's governmental counterparts. He continually makes reference to United Nations Security Council Resolution 242. This was the resolution that called for Israel to withdraw its troops from occupied territories after the 1967 Six-Day War.

BEYOND THE WHITE HOUSE (2007)

In this work Carter goes into great detail to examine the work of the Carter Center, focusing on two areas. He and his team have gone to several countries to monitor elections. His work has led to mixed success, because he must deal with corrupt officials, such as Manuel Noriega in Panama, and Fidel Castro in Cuba. Carter discusses his cooperation with sitting US Presidents as well as the United Nations High Commissioner for Human Rights and the International Red Cross. Members of the center, as well as Carter and his wife Rosalynn, have traveled extensively to Africa to offer aid to impoverished countries who are dealing with poor sanitary conditions, disease and malnutrition. Some critics have labeled this as a work of an unpopular former one-term president trying to establish a legacy as peacemaker, using the cachet of his brokering a Middle East Peace Accord and receiving the Nobel Prize. In this narrative, it appears that some of the foreign governments believe that Carter and the Carter Center are acting in an official capacity as an arm of the United States government. While Carter goes to great lengths to inform his audience that he contacts the incumbent President and the

State Department before taking any action, that is not always the case. Perhaps the most revealing comment Carter made while being interviewed by Barbara Walters speaks volumes about his feelings. "By far the best years are those I'm enjoying now since Rosalyn and I left the White House."

A CALL TO ACTION – WOMEN, RELIGION, VIOLENCE AND POWER (2014)

This work focuses on such diverse issues as human trafficking, spouse abuse, honor killings, child marriages, sexual assault and rape. As part of Carter Center initiatives, the former president and his wife visited more than 100 countries. Carter was appalled by the violence and discrimination against women. Some of the abuses he uncovered were based in religious customs. Carter challenged world leaders to make a concerted effort to do more to end the poor treatment of women and the denial of basic human rights.[5]

FAITH - A JOURNEY FOR ALL (2018)

Faith- A Journey for All, published in 2018, was a *New York Times* bestseller. It dealt with the topic of faith in success as well as in disappointment. Carter noted: "My primary goal (in the book) is to explore the broadest meaning of faith, its far-reaching effect on our lives, and its relationship to past, present and future events in America and around the world."[6]

In *Faith*, Carter reflects on his Baptist heritage and his understanding of the Abrahamic faiths—Judaism, Christianity, and Islam. He also discusses the personal impact of his sister Ruth Carter Stapleton, who was an evangelist. He further writes about his partnership with God and how his relationship with faith manifested itself in the various stages of his life: as a midshipman at the Naval Academy, as a farmer, as the governor of Georgia, as President of the United States, and as a Nobel Prize recipient. He frequently refers to the writings of theologians whom he admires: Richard Niebur, Dietrich Bonhoffer, and Soren Kierkegaard. In looking at the present and future generations, Carter asks the rhetorical question: "Can the moral values of democracy, freedom, justice, equality and compassion be transmitted to a next generation without religious faith? I hope so, but I am confident that religious faith enhances the possibility of that transmission."[7]

Carter concludes that he is optimistic about the future, but he is ever mindful of what is happening to American society. He makes reference to issues like climate change, the gun lobby, and the lack of collegiality in Congress. He writes: "The collective guidance of the American people will shape the future of our nation, but we must retain our own self-confidence, and faith in basic principles like truth, equality, justice, peace, democracy and mutual respect even between citizens who disagree on controversial issues."[8] Carter feels that despite all of our shortcomings, Americans still have faith in their country and can handle the many unmet challenges.

The endnotes of *Faith* indicate that this was Carter's thirtieth work, but that list includes the publication of his Nobel Prize acceptance speech, which is not really a book. As Carter is now 95 at this printing, and challenged with a wide range of health issues, one cannot tell if this will be Carter's last book.

THE OTHER SIDE OF JIMMY CARTER

During his literary career, Carter occasionally branched out from his political and faith-based works to explore the genres of poetry and fiction. *Always a Reckoning and Other Poems*, was published in 1995. It is an illustrated volume of his verse, an anthology containing forty-four poems. Noted scholar and author Douglas Brinkley said: "The extent to which this is a tribute is a matter of taste, but certainly could be worse—that Carter's poems were an amalgam of Carl Sandberg at his worst and Rod McKuen at his best."[9] In this work the former President wrote about people he knew. He also wrote poems about his youth, about Plains and peanuts, about politics, and the private lives of his family, especially his wife Rosalynn. Carter was not the first president to publish a book of poetry. Presidents John Quincy Adams and Abraham Lincoln were both poets and had their works published. Carter's seventeen-year-old granddaughter, Sarah Elizabeth Chuldenko, drew the illustrations for *Always a Reckoning and Other Poems*. The poem "Plains" is Carter's musing about his hometown.

PLAINS

"Pioneering White Men fought to claim
the land of Indians they sent west to die.
Our families moved in then to occupy
the rolling plains that gave the town its name
There were only half a thousand souls,
White and black, the master and the slave
Neither side forgot nor ever gave
Each other ways to reach their common goals"[10]

Jimmy Carter used the focus in many of his later books to promote the Carter Center, an institution that he and Rosalynn developed to create global projects for the good of disadvantaged nations. Readers can find the center mentioned in *Faith*, *After the White House*, as well as *Palestine Peace not Apartheid.*

Carter's philosophy of the center was that it is "easier to wage war than to wage peace." The former President served as a mediator or negotiator in areas of global conflict, especially in national elections. He played a significant role in promoting free elections in Haiti in 1990. Researchers from the Carter Center aim to bring to public awareness many of the human rights issues that beset our world. Today at age 95, Carter is still a global advocate for world peace. He seems to have found his niche in the world as a peacemaker and preacher. For more information about the goals of the Carter Center, please refer to Appendix II.

---

[1] Stuart E. Eizenstat. *President Carter: The White House Years.* (New York: St Martin's Press, 2018). 20
[2] Douglas Brinkley. *The Unfinished Presidency: Jimmy Carter's Journey Beyond the White House.* (New York: Viking Press, 1999.). xix
[3] Kathryn Moore. *American Presidents: A Complete History.* (New York: Fall River Press, 2007). 739.
[4] Review by Peter Preston, *The Guardian*, October 16, 2004
[5] Cartercenter.org. March 16, 2014. (Accessed January 20, 2020)

[6] Jimmy Carter. *Faith: A Journey for All.* (New York: Simon & Schuster, 2015). 30.
[7] *Ibid.*, pp. 52-53.
[8] *Ibid.*, p. 121.
[9] Max.J. Skidmore. *After the White House: Former Presidents as Private Citizens.* (New York: Palgrave MacMillan, 2004). 246.
[10] Jimmy Carter. *Always a Reckoning and Other Poems.* (New York: Time Books, 1995.) 37.

CHAPTER SEVEN
THE FATHER AND SON PRESIDENTS

[Boston: published by n. Dearborn, between 1814 and 1852] Photograph.
https://www.loc.gov/item/97519595

John Adams
Born: October 30, 1735- Braintree, Massachusetts
Died: July 4, 1826- Quincy, Massachusetts
Second President of the United States
Term: 1798-1801
Wife: Abigail Smith
Political Party: Federalist
Undergraduate College- Harvard College

"Wisdom and knowledge, as well as virtue, diffused generally among the body of people are necessary for the preservation of their rights and liberties." (from the Massachusetts State Constitution, written by John Adams.)

John Adams, the first Vice President of the United States and the first US Ambassador to the Court of St James, was an eloquent speaker and a prolific letter writer. He was the first president who was a graduate of Harvard College. Adams was the father of future president John Quincy Adams, a distinction that remained until the elections of George Herbert Walker Bush and George W. Bush almost 200 years later. He was the only founding father who never owned slaves.

As for his writings, we have his grandson Charles Francis Adams to thank for preserving his writings, editing them and compiling them into a book titled *The Works of John Adams, Second President of the United States: A life of the Author, Notes and Illustrations.* The work, which consists of ten volumes, was published in 1856 in Boston by Little, Brown and Company. It is a repository of Adams' writings. Included in this collection is an autobiography that was originally written for distribution to family members rather than to the general public.

Some of Adams's early works include the drafting of the Massachusetts state constitution and the 1765 document "A Dissertation on the Canon and Feudal Law." Another of his notable early works was *Discourses on Davisa: A Survey of Papers on Political History* (1790). It was published in The Gazette of the United States in 1805.

***THOUGHTS ON GOVERNMENT* (1776)**

The full title of this 30-page essay was originally *Thoughts on Government Applicable to the Present State of the American Colonies.* Originally, this document was introduced as a pamphlet, one that Adams was reluctant to take ownership of. It was fellow signer of the Declaration of Independence, Dr. Benjamin Rush, who attributed the work to Adams.

Adams outlines the concept of three branches of government designed to create a system of checks and balances. Those branches were the executive, legislative, and judicial. Throughout his political life, Adams was a proponent of a strong central government. With this document—along with his drafting of the Massachusetts Constitution—Adams unknowingly was helping to shape American political thought. These beliefs and political philosophies would eventually come into conflict with those of Thomas Jefferson and Alexander Hamilton.

Adams originally penned *Thoughts* in response to a request from the North Carolina legislature, which sought his expertise in drafting their provincial constitution. "We ought to consider what is the end of government, before we determine which is the best form. Upon this point all speculative politicians will agree, that the happiness of society is the end of government, as all divines and moral philosophers will agree that the happiness of the individual is the end of man. From this principle it will follow that the form of government which communicates ease, comfort, security, or, in one word, happiness, to the greatest number of persons, and in the greatest degree, is the best."[1]

THE WRITINGS OF JOHN ADAMS

Between 1802 and 1807 John Adams began to put down on paper, his life story. His autobiography was well over 400 pages. This three-volume set included letters, essays, public documents and drafts. (Published by the Library of America. edited by Gordon S Wood- Professor of History- Brown University)

Adams was a prolific letter writer and there were over 1000 letters written between him and his wife, Abigail. (See My *Dearest Friend: Letters of Abigail and John Adams,* Cambridge, Massachusetts, Harvard University Press 2007- edited by Margaret Hogan)

College professors have edited many of the recent compilations of Adams's original writings. They have created their own introductions and prefaces to analyze Adams's works and to provide independent interpretations and commentary.

(Library of Congress, Prints and Photographic Division
https://www.loc.gov/item/2003677894/

John Quincy Adams
Born: July 11, 1767- Braintree, Massachusetts
Died: February 23, 1848- Washington, DC
Sixth President of the United States
Term: 1825-1829
Wife: Louisa Johnson
Political Party: Federalist, Democratic-Republican
Undergraduate University: Harvard College

"The best guarantee against the abuse of power consists in the freedom, the purity, and the frequency of popular elections."
-John Quincy Adams Inaugural Address, March 4,1825

As the son of a United States president, John Quincy Adams had a front-row seat as to the workings of American government and especially foreign relations. The younger Adams accompanied his father on a transatlantic voyage to Paris. It is not really surprising that he was appointed to the position of Minister to the Netherlands at age 26. In 1802, he was elected to the United States Senate from Massachusetts. In 1808, President James Madison appointed him as Minister to Russia. Adams also helped to negotiate and draft the Treaty of Ghent in 1814 that formally ended the War of 1812. During the administration of James Monroe, Adams served as Secretary of State from 1817 to 1825. With that pedigree, John Quincy Adams was primed to become President of the United States.

That ascension, however, was not an easy one. Since no candidate in the election achieved the majority of electoral votes, this election was decided in the House of Representatives.

John Quincy Adams began his writing career by maintaining a diary while traveling in Europe with his father. At one point he wanted to pursue a career in writing.

Adams was an avid reader and a great lover of poetry. At one time he mused about becoming a poet himself. According to an article by David Odegard that appeared in Buzzfeed on February 17, 2014, Adams's favorite book was *Oberon*, a German fairytale poem, by Christoph Martin Wieland. Adams took it upon himself to translate the work into English.

***PUBLICOLA* (1792)**

The 1792 work, *Publicola*, was comprised of a series of letters that were Adams's observations on Thomas Paine's *Rights of Man*. *Publicola* was John Quincy Adams's pen name for this work as he wished to publish this work anonymously. These letters reveal Adams's views of the early days of the French Revolution as well as the British Constitution. He is quite critical of Paine's work and further explores Paine's view of American constitutional theory.

***LETTERS ON FREEMASONRY* (1833)**

Neither John Quincy Adams nor his father were freemasons, although thirteen US Presidents have been, including George Washington and, most recently, Gerald R. Ford. This secretive organization has, over the years, been accused of conspiracy theories. Adams was a member of the Anti-Masonic Party, one of the first third parties in the United States.

Letters on Freemasonry is a compilation of letters written after the mysterious disappearance and death of William Morgan. Morgan was a former mason who threatened to divulge the secrets of freemasonry in a book. It was believed that disgruntled masons murdered Morgan.

Adams weighed in on this issue. "To all members of the masonic fraternity who entered it before the murder of Morgan, I would extend the most liberal Toleration. Most of them took the Oaths without reflecting upon what they imported.... Now the case is otherwise. How they can now take or administer the cutthroat Oath to keep Secret, what all the world knows, I cannot comprehend."[2]

WANTS OF MAN (1840)

This work is comprised of poems of religion and society, going back to Adams's early interest in poetry. Below is an excerpt from one of the poems from this work.

"Man wants but little here below,
Nor wants that little long."
'Tis not with me exactly so;
But 'tis so in the song.
My wants are many and, if told,
Would muster many a score;
And were each wish a mint of gold,
I still should long for more."[3]

(From Bliss Carmen et.al., eds. *The World's Best Poetry. Vol. VI,* Fancy: Sentiment. Philadelphia: John D. Morris and Company. 1904)

Of all of the writings of John Quincy Adams, it appears that he chose not to write about his father and his presidency. Centuries later, President George W. Bush would decide that he would write a biography about his father, George Herbert Walker Bush, and his life and presidency. So we have *41- a Portrait of My Father*, as the one literary offering of a son who served as chief executive writing about his father, who was also a chief executive.

(Library of Congress Prints and Photographic Division, LC-USZ262-9830)

George Herbert Walker Bush
Born: June 12, 1924- Milton, Massachusetts
Died: November 30, 2018- Houston, Texas
41st President of the United States
Term: 1989-1993
Wife: Barbara Pierce
Political Party: Republican
Undergraduate College: Yale University

"Some see leadership as high drama and the sound of the trumpets calling and sometimes it is that. But I see history as a book with many pages, and each day we fill a pages with acts of helpfulness and meaning." (Inaugural speech, January 20,1989)

George Bush had all of the credentials and an outstanding resume to be President of the United States. Born to a prominent New England family and son of a United States Senator, Bush was educated in private schools and received his undergraduate degree from Yale University. He served as a navy pilot during World War II and was the last president to be a war veteran. Prior to his election as president, Bush served as a member of the House of Representatives, U.S. Representative to the United Nations, Ambassador to China, and director of the Central Intelligence Agency (CIA). In 1980, he was chosen as Ronald Reagan's running mate. After two terms as Vice-President, Bush was elected President in his own right in 1988.

Bush lacked the interest in writing books that many of his fellow chief executives had and was a reluctant author. On the other hand, he enjoyed writing letters. He had stated on several occasions that he was not really interested in writing his autobiography. Bush would leave that endeavor to those who would ultimately judge him. It was his son, George W. Bush, who would write the personal tribute biography of his father. As early as 1977, Bush was approached by George Champion of the Economic Development Council of New York and was asked tor write a book based on his experiences as director of the CIA. That project never materialized.

LOOKING FORWARD (1988)

Despite his reluctance, George H.W. Bush was the author of four books. His first was *Looking Forward,* which he used to launch his run for the presidency in 1988. He had no qualms in letting everyone know that author Victor Gold was going to be his ghostwriter for this work. "I asked my good friend and great writer Vic Gold to ghostwrite sort of a 'political' autobiography, and the kind of book that comes out about the candidate during an election year."[4]

Written while still Vice President, this book explores Bush's previous careers: war veteran, Texas oil man and politician. Bush examines major players in the US and on the international scene, such as Ronald Reagan, Henry Kissinger, and Richard Nixon. He also delves into his personal life, sharing the tragedy of his daughter's struggle with leukemia as well as his relationship with Barbara. Upon publication, this work shared its proceeds with the United Negro College Fund and an organization dedicated to leukemia research.

A WORLD TRANSFORMED (1998)

Co-written with his National Security Advisor Brent Scowcroft, *A World Transformed* presents Bush's reflections on foreign relations during his presidency. The duo discusses the end of the Cold War, the collapse of the Soviet Union and the US relationship with Mikhail Gorbachev. They also write about the impact of the Gulf War, the re-unification of Germany, and the Tiananmen Square uprising. Bush makes the case for the invasion of Baghdad and the effort to remove Saddam Hussein from power in

1991. They were concerned about a possible shift in the balance of power in the Persian Gulf.

Michael Beschloss, writing in *Newsweek* Magazine, commented: "In a strong new book, the ex-president recalls dangerous days…It should leave little doubt how lucky we were that we had such a seasoned hand on the tiller at a time when foreign policy really counted." The book demonstrates how personalities and relationships truly made a difference in diplomacy.

ALL THE BEST: MY LIFE IN LETTERS AND OTHER WRITING (1999)

The best known of Bush's books is *All the Best: My Life in Letters and Other Writing*. This book was originally published in 1999 and was re-issued thirteen years later. Bush had a reputation for being a prodigious letter writer. The book includes letters written to his father while he was away at school, as well as letters to his then girlfriend Barbara Pierce, who eventually became his wife and First Lady. Many of the included documents came from the George H. W. Bush Presidential Library in College Station, Texas.

The book did become a *New York Times* bestseller; his editor asked him to add a seventeenth chapter thirteen years later as a postscript to the original work. Bush was 88 years old at the time. He requested that the proceeds from the sale of this updated version be donated to the Bush School of Government and Public Service at Texas A and M University. It would be left to his son, George W. Bush, to write a true biography as well as a tribute to his father.

SPEAKING OF FREEDOM (2009)

Speaking of Freedom is a book of the collected speeches of President George Herbert Walker Bush. The 42 speeches include Bush's acceptance speech for the Republican nomination for President in 1988. The George Bush Presidential Library Foundation copyrighted the book. Also included in this volume are commencement addresses to several colleges and, more notably, his announcement that he was deploying troops to Saudi Arabia, and a later speech regarding the Persian Gulf War. Bush also inserts a speech he gave upon his signing of the Americans with Disabilities Act of 1990.

Although George H.W. Bush was a reticent historian and shied away from the spotlight after his term of office ended, he continued to be a prolific letter writer. Those notes and letters provide us with an insight and perspective into the life and career of one of the twentieth century's major players on the world stage.

(Credit to Eric Draper, photographer, courtesy of the George Bush Presidential Library.)

George W. Bush
Born: 1946- New Haven, Connecticut
43rd President of the United States
Term: 2001-2009
Wife: Laura Welch
Political Party: Republican
Undergraduate College: Yale University

Only twice in the history of this country have a father and son both served as President of the United States. The first were John Adams (2) and John Quincy Adams (6). More recently we had George Herbert Walker Bush (41) and George W. Bush (43). The latter Bush, a two- term president, will ultimately have a great deal to write about but, like many of his predecessors, his first book would be a "get to know me" work, designed to gain him national exposure in preparation for a White House run.

A CHARGE TO KEEP (1999)

George Bush's first book, *A Charge to Keep,* was first published in 1999 while Bush was Governor of Texas. The work ultimately became the springboard for his presidential campaign, and in subsequent editions the phrase "My Journey to the White House" was added to the cover. In this book, which became a bestseller, Bush candidly examines his experiences, both personal as well as political, and describes for the reader how these experiences created the values that led him to the decision to run for President of the United States. “Most lives have defining moments. Moments that forever change you. Moments that set you on a different course. Moments of recognition so vivid and so clear that everything later seems different.”[5]

DECISION POINTS (2010)

Bush’s memoirs were published two years after his term of office ended. The rollout of *Decision Points* coincided with the groundbreaking for the George W. Bush Presidential Library and Museum located on the campus of Southern Methodist University in Dallas, Texas. Book sales exceeded of two million copies in less than two months after its release. The 487-page work appeared as number one on *The New York Times* Bestseller list as soon as it was published. The only other memoir that came close to this level of interest was President Bill Clinton’s book, *My Life*. Bush’s *Decision Points* was written with the help of Christopher Michel, a former White House Director of Speech Writing.

The early chapters of this work were devoted to Bush’s tenure as governor of Texas. Later chapters examined some pivotal events during his presidency. They included the terrorist attacks on September 11, 2001, and the wars in Iraq and Afghanistan. Domestically, the former President reviewed his No Child Left Behind educational strategy; dealing with the aftermath of Hurricane Katrina, which devastated the city of New Orleans; and, of course, the notorious presidential election of 2000. Bush also revealed how he faced a moral dilemma when dealing with the issue of stem cell research.

While many skeptics believed that Bush was not an avid reader, in *Decision Points*, he often cites other books that had an influence on his presidency. Two specifically mentioned were *Supreme Command* by Eliot Cohen and *Dereliction of Duty*, written by former general and National Security Advisor H.R. McMaster.

REVIEWS

Decision Points was met with mixed reviews, and apparently the book-buying public paid little or no attention. Most memoirs by former presidents are designed to reshape and reframe their administrations and try to preserve their legacy in a positive light. George W. Bush's book was no different.

"George W. Bush's memoir *Decision Points* could well have been titled 'The Decider Decides': it's an autobiography focused around 'the most consequential decisions' of his presidency and his personal life, from his decision to give up drinking in 1986 to his decision to invade Iraq in 2003 to his decisions regarding the financial crisis of 2008. It is a book that is part spin, part mea culpa, part family scrapbook, part self-conscious effort to (re) shape his political legacy."[6]

Goodreads is a social media site for book reviews and recommendations with an extensive database. The reviewers at *Goodreads* had this opinion about *Decision Points*:

"...the failure to bring Osama bin Laden to justice ranks as his biggest disappointment and... his success in denying the terrorists their fondest wish—attacking America again—is among his proudest achievements."

"A groundbreaking new brand of presidential memoir, *Decision Points* will captivate supporters, surprise critics, and change perspectives on eight remarkable years in American history—and on the man at the center of events."[7]

However, *Goodreads* did nominate *Decision Poin*ts for one of its awards for best autobiography.

The Los Angeles Times review made this significant observation. It noted:

"Decision Points confirms many of the better nonfiction accounts of his presidency published while he was in office, particularly Bob Woodward's four volumes and Robert Draper's *Dead Certain*. The Bush White House may not have been given to doubts or its chief executive to indecision, but it did have a penchant for ad hoc deliberation, stubborn persistence in the face of failure—as in Iraq up to the surge—excessive personal loyalty and for being 'blind-sided' by events beyond the unforeseeable tragedy of 9/11."[8]

41- *A Portrait of My Father* (2014)

Noted author and historian David McCullough's daughter, Dorie, had suggested to President George W. Bush that he should write about his father. She said that her father lamented the fact that there had been no serious work written about John Quincy Adams, the son of the second US President, John Adams. So, in homage to his father, Bush 43 penned, *41- A Portrait of My Father*, which was published in 2014. Bush observed that the work was less of an historical treatise and more of a love story.

Ann Compton of *The Washington Post* made these comments in her review of the book: "Indeed, '41' is a chronicle of family love and loss, written in a plainspoken voice that sounds just like George W. Bush in person, with wisecrack asides and loads of family sentimentality. For those of us who watched both Bush presidencies up close, the book is also a predictably firm defense of the elder Bush's foreign policy, particularly in Iraq and the Cold War."[9]

PORTRAITS OF COURAGE: A COMMANDER-IN CHIEF'S TRIBUTE TO AMERICA'S WARRIORS (2017)

George W. Bush's most recent book, published in 2017, highlights his paintings, the hobby he took up in his retirement. The George W. Bush Institute has initiated a military service initiative, and the former president has created a volume of 66 full-color portraits of members of the US Military that have served our country since the terrorist attacks on 9/11. Each of the selected paintings includes the inspirational story of the veteran. Bush hopes that this book, in some way, will help pay tribute and honor the sacrifices that these individuals made. President Bush has indicated that he will donate the net proceeds of this book to the George W. Bush Presidential Center in Dallas, Texas. This non-profit organization helps post 9/11 veterans to transition to civilian life. *Portraits of Courage* became both a *New York Times* bestseller and an Amazon Best Book of the Month.

George W. Bush can still have a great deal to write about. Whether expressed in his art or his words, the forty-third President of the United States had a front-row seat to observe American politics as both the son of a distinguished diplomat and president and as president himself, one who got thrust into the public spotlight with the election of 2000 and the necessity to come to grips with the tragedy of September 11, 2001. Future books by Bush about his administration, his family, or his philanthropies may show up on bookstore shelves in the future.

---

[1] John Adams. *Thoughts on Government Applicable to the Present State of the American Colonies*. (Philadelphia: John Dunlap, 1776). 1

[2] Letter from Congressman John Quincy Adams to Stephen Bates, Washington, D.C. April 1, 1833.)

[3] from Bliss Carmen et.al.eds. *The World's Best Poetry.* Vol. VI Fancy: Sentiment. Philadelphia: John D. Morris and Company, 1904)

[4] George H.W. Bush. *All the Best: My Life in Letters and Other Writings*.
(New York: Scribner, 2013). 351.

[5] George W. Bush and Michael Herskowitz. *A Charge to Keep.* (New York: William Morrow and Company, Inc., 1999). 1.

[6] fr. Michiko Kakutani, "In Bush Memoir, Policy Intersects with Personality" *New York Times,* November 3, 2010, accessed 9/11/19).

[7] (Goodreads.com accessed 9/11/19)

[8] (Tim Rutten, *Los Angeles Times* 3/12/14, accessed 9/11/19

[9] book review- *The Washington Post,* November 13, 2014. Accessed 1/7/2020)

Chapter Eight
America's First Baby-Boomer President

(Photo courtesy of the Library of Congress, Prints and Photographic Division, Washington, DC)

William Jefferson (Bill) Clinton
Born: August 19, 1946- Hope, Arkansas
Political Party- Democrat
42nd President
Term: 1993-2001
Wife: Hillary Rodham
Undergraduate College- Georgetown University
Favorite Read: "*Meditations*" by Marcus Aurelius (Buzzfeed article.)

"America promises liberty but demands civic responsibility. America promises the opportunity to pursue happiness but does not guarantee it."

Bill Clinton possessed the ability to connect with people at a most basic level. He wrote only one book prior to his first presidential election in 1992, *Putting People First.* Since then he has been able to cash in on his cachet as chief executive to develop an audience and write about topics that he wanted to. He is not a writer of history and politics like Theodore Roosevelt or Woodrow Wilson. Nor is he the zealous faith-based author like Jimmy Carter.

PUTTING PEOPLE FIRST: HOW WE ALL CHANGE AMERICA (WITH AL GORE. 1992)

This is Clinton's first book and the one published by the presidential candidate and his running mate, Senator Al Gore of Tennessee, to launch their 1992 presidential campaign. The topics covered spell out the candidates' platforms in the following areas: the economy, crime, education, the environment, energy, health care, housing, national security, business, the space program, trade, and welfare.

BETWEEN HOPE AND HISTORY (1996)

This book, published by Random House in September 1996, was essentially a pep talk to the citizenry of the United States, outlining for prospective voters, Clinton's accomplishments during his first four years in office and his visions for a second term. He is the incumbent here and seeks a shared vision for America for the 21st century.

Between Hope and History is divided into three parts: Opportunity, Responsibility, and Community. Opportunity for all Americans; Responsibility from all Americans and the forging of stronger American community. The President believed that these were the three values that shaped the character of the American people.

"Opportunity is only half of America's basic bargain. The other half is responsibility."[1]

Clinton spends a great deal of time discussing Social Security, Medicare and Medicaid and how the country should prepare to pay for these programs in the future. He illustrates how his administration was able to reduce the federal deficit.

"Our founders created a nation, as Lincoln said 'conceived in liberty.' But they understood something many Americans forget: Freedom works only when it is exercised with responsibility."[2]

Other topics covered in this work include the importance of education, the role of families, and the relationship between business and government.

Unlike the dubious authorship of books written by other presidents, Clinton acknowledges assistance in writing this book. He mentions William E. Nothdurft, an author and public policy consultant, as well as Joellyn Murphy, his researcher, as being primarily responsible for creating the draft of this book.

During that re-election bid, Clinton was able to get civil rights icon Rosa Parks to accompany him on a whistle-stop campaign tour, a story that he certainly could have used to his advantage in his book. In the area of human rights, while the initial planning and preparation for a national Holocaust Museum and Memorial began back in 1979, President Clinton was front and center for the museum's dedication and opening on April 22, 1993. For whatever reason, he chose not to address these issues in any of his writings.

MY LIFE- BILL CLINTON (2004)

This work is Clinton's autobiography. It became a best seller and has sold over two million copies. The Knopf division of Random House had offered him an advance of $10 million for his memoirs. Clinton hired Dr. Edward L. (Ted) Widmer, a history professor at Washington College in Maryland, and former Clinton White House Special Assistant, to research and compile documents, data and stories from Clinton's two terms as Chief Executive, to be used in the creation of this book.[3]

This 957-page tome is a candid look at Clinton's life, both personal as well as political. In the early chapters, Clinton discusses in detail his youth in Hope, Arkansas, including that he never knew his biological father, who was killed in an accident before he was born. He writes in a conversational style that is easily understandable, but he gets bogged down in the details.

The second half of the book deals with Clinton's political career. He discusses his dealings with Newt Gingrich, who was Speaker of the House during his administration. He is proud of his efforts to achieve peace in the Middle East by bringing together Yitzhak Rabin and Yasser Arafat for the famous handshake on the White House lawn. Clinton analyzes his unsuccessful efforts to develop a health care plan for America. True to his goal, the former President reviews his impeachment as well as his troubled relationship with Monica Lewinsky. He shares some choice comments about Kenneth Starr, special prosecutor appointed to investigate Clinton and whose report ultimately led to his impeachment.

Upon his first election to the presidency in 1992, Clinton asked the rhetorical question: "How did Americans come to choose their first baby-boom President, the third youngest in history, only the second governor of a small state, carrying more baggage than an ocean liner?"[4] What was the reason Clinton had just upended the incumbent, President George H.W. Bush? Everyone knew it was the economy.

The epilogue of *My Life* is the author's somber reflection on his life, both personal and political. "…I'm still working on that list of life goals I made as a young man. Becoming a good person is a lifelong effort that required letting go of anger at others and holding on to responsibility for the mistakes I've made. And it requires forgiveness."[5]

In the years after his presidency, Bill Clinton decided that after doing well, he believed he had a moral obligation to do good for both the community and the world and to make amends for his past indiscretions. He and Hillary then established the Clinton Foundation in 1997. Headquartered in New York City, the Foundation has sponsored a number of global initiatives focused on such issues as world health and climate change. It is not surprising then, that a number of Clinton's later writings included a field guide for volunteerism and helping others as well as an analysis of what his administration did for the economy and what has happened since he left office.

GIVING: HOW EACH OF US CAN CHANGE THE WORLD (2007)

President Clinton was very proud of the Clinton Foundation and its accomplishments, although not to the extent that Jimmy Carter extolls the virtues of the Carter Center. Clinton's book *Giving: How Each of Us Can Change the World* (2007) encourages readers to get engaged in philanthropic endeavors. This is Clinton's call to action in his post-presidential world. Those who can, he states, should give financially. For those who cannot, he suggests that Americans offer to volunteer time to worthwhile endeavors. Clinton was given an advance of $6 million for this book, $1 million of which he donated to charity.

According to Joe Conason, author of *Man of the World*: "The purpose of the book was to 'democratize CGI (Clinton Global Initiative)' by creating a new inspirational platform for citizen philanthropy from the lemonade stand to the sustainable corporation."[6]

Within the 240 pages, Clinton shares stories of people from all walks of life who have made it their business to help those, both in the United States and around the world, with resources that will improve their lives. Clinton observes that disasters of many kinds face our world. He believes that we need to develop and hone our giving skills. His message is similar to that of former President Jimmy Carter, who believes that such humanitarian acts will lead us to a worthy life. Clinton notes: "We all have the capacity to do great things. My hope is that the people and stories of this book will lift spirits, touch hearts, and demonstrate that citizen activism and service can be a powerful change in the world."[7]

The book launch for *Giving* took place on September 5, 2007, in a gymnasium in Harlem, under the auspices of a local non-profit organization, not the glitz and glamour of a more traditional New York book launch. The day before the book's coming out, Clinton appeared on the Oprah Winfrey Show. *Giving* became a number one bestseller on *The New York Times* list with an initial press run of 750,000 copies.[8]

BACK TO WORK: WHY WE NEED A STRONG GOVERNMENT FOR A STRONG ECONOMY (2011)

Back to Work provides Clinton's views on the challenges facing the US today and why government matters. Those challenges include job creation, dealing with the mortgage crisis and financial responsibility. Clinton encourages the government and the private sector to work together to build a strong economy. He wrote of several bad governmental policies and the anti-governmentalism that had begun to pervade the political landscape. The former president observed that we need a "smart government" to recruit and keep *New York Times* people in the workforce to continue to stimulate the economy after the 2009 recession. The book," expressed the dissatisfaction he had felt for well over a year with the president (Obama) and other Democratic leaders for failing to fight back against the Tea Party…"[9]

The reviews of *Back to Work* were mixed. *New York Times* book critic Michiko Kakutani wrote in her review: "Readers would find a lucid one-man rebuttal of the Tea Party's anti-government agenda. A series of shrewd talking points for Democrats trying to hold on to the White House…. A self-serving reminder of the prosperity the country enjoyed during Mr. Clinton's tenure in the White House, meant to burnish his legacy."[10]

Clinton's book, when published, appeared at number four on *The New York Times* nonfiction bestseller list.

THE PRESIDENT IS MISSING – A NOVEL - WITH JAMES PATTERSON (2018.)

Clinton partnered with acclaimed mystery writer James Patterson to develop a plot centered on the presidency and the White House. The story line takes place over a matter of a few days. This novel of over 500 pages, published by Little Brown, and Company, became a bestseller. He is only the second president to author a novel, the first being Jimmy Carter, who wrote *The Hornet's Nest*, a novel set during the time of the American Revolution.

REVIEWS OF *THE PRESIDENT IS MISSING*

Critics of this joint effort were more bemused by the book than impressed by it. Anthony Lane, a reviewer for the *New Yorker* wrote: "Bill Clinton, who can write, has hooked up with James Patterson, who can't, but whose works have sold more than three hundred and seventy-five million copies, most of them to happy and contented customers for whom good writing would only get in the way."[11]

Ron Charles of *The Washington Post* observed: "For much of *The President is Missing* Patterson seems to have deferred to the First Writer."[12] He went on to assure readers that there was no breech of national security in the book. "*The President is Missing* reveals as many secrets about the U.S. Government as 'The Pink Panther' reveals about the French government."[13]

Bill Clinton has a gift for writing, and he is a consummate and engaging storyteller.

As he is relatively young for a former president and enjoys being in the public spotlight, readers may not be finished hearing from Bill Clinton. We can probably expect new writings in the future. He may even team up again with another author. Because their first collaborative effort was so successful, Bill Clinton and James Patterson have announced a second novel, *The President's Daughter*, which will be published in June, 2021.

---

[1] Bill Clinton. *Between Hope and History*
(New York: Random House, 1996). 58.
[2] *Ibid.*, pp. 61-62
[3] Joe Conason. *Man of the World: The Further Endeavors of Bill Clinton*
(New York: Simon & Schuster, 2016). 134-136.
[4] Bill Clinton. *My Life*
(New York: Alfred A. Knopf, 2005). 445.
[5] *Ibid.*, p. 956.
[6] Conason, p. 287.
[7] Bill Clinton. *Giving: How Each of us can Change the World.*
(New York: Alfred A. Knopf, 2007).
[8] Conason, pp. 287-288
[9] *Ibid.*, p. 373.
[10] *Ibid.*
[11] Anthony Lane, *The New Yorker*, June 5, 2018. Accessed February 14, 2020.
[12] Ron Charles, "Bill Clinton and James Patterson's The President is Missing is an
Awkward Duet" *The Washington Post*. June 4, 2018. Accessed February 14, 2020.
[13] *Ibid.*

CHAPTER NINE
PRESIDENTS OF THE TWENTY-FIRST CENTURY

(Library of Congress Prints and Photographic Division, LC-DIG-ppbd-00358)

Barak Obama
Born: August 4, 1961- Honolulu, Hawaii
44th President of the United States
Term: 2009-2017
Wife: Michelle Robinson
Political Party: Democrat
Undergraduate College: Columbia University
Nobel Peace Prize Recipient- 2009

"All men live in the shadow of their fathers—the more distant the father the deeper the shadow."[1] Barack Obama, *Dreams From my Father.*

"'We hold these truths to be self-evident.' *In those words, I hear the spirit of Douglass and Delany, as well as Jefferson and Lincoln; the struggles of Martin and Malcolm and unheralded marchers to bring these words to life.*"[2]

One hundred and forty-five years after the signing of the Emancipation Proclamation and 44 years after the Civil Rights Act was passed, the people of the United States elected the first African-American president. Born in Hawaii, Barack Obama had been a community organizer and United States Senator from Illinois when he burst onto the national stage with his stirring address at the Democratic National Convention in 2004. Viewers knew that Obama was an engaging speaker, and his rise to prominence encouraged the public to read his books.

DREAMS FROM MY FATHER (1995)

Barak Obama wrote his autobiography at the very young age of 34, well before he became a political figure in American politics. He was a recent Harvard Law School graduate at the time, well before the meteoric rise in his political career. *Dreams from My Father: A Story of Race and Inheritance* was first published in 1995 and republished in 2004, when it hit *The New York Times* Bestseller list. The book examines the events in his early life, from growing up in Honolulu and Chicago to his entry into law school. Obama noted that: "Originally the book was going to be a series of essays on issues of race and class, but as it evolved, it's become a memoir of my family and my experiences as an organizer."[3]

In the summer of 2004 Obama delivered the keynote speech at the Democratic National Convention in Boston, which provided entrée onto the nation-wide television scene. With the publishing of this book and his second work, *The Audacity of Hope*, Obama established himself as a legitimate and gifted author. There are many who believe he is among the best writers of all of the Presidents. It is partly for this reason that Obama and his wife Michelle were offered such a huge literary deal to publish their autobiographies.

Barack Obama was the product of an interracial marriage of a black African father and a white mother from the Midwest. His first literary effort has been labeled a memoir, an autobiography, and a family history. Whatever way the reader chooses to view this retrospective, Obama sought to define his role in the world, which culture to identify with and how to focus his future. *Dreams from My Father* is divided into three sections: Origins, Chicago, and Kenya. Readers who took this book to heart got a unique opportunity to see the true Barack Obama, well before the handlers and the American political process attempted to shape him into a viable and electable presidential contender.

In one section, Barack (also known as Barry) examines his experiences as a community organizer in Chicago, Illinois. He worked at the Altgeld Gardens housing project. He expresses his disillusionment with what he saw and how so many of the people he met were downtrodden and had a feeling of hopelessness about the condition of African-Americans in their city. The men and women Obama came in contact with felt they were being manipulated as political pawns of the Chicago Democratic Party machine. Party and government officials made promises for civic improvements that were never kept. Obama vividly describes a war-torn landscape of potholes, backed-up sewers, abandoned lots and no jobs. He called it "the deathly smell of failure."

Obama specifically mentions the impact on the community by Nation of Islam leader Louis Farrakhan, with a number of men and women becoming Muslim in desperation. He also mentions Farrakhan's newspaper, *The Final Call*, which spews forth a daily screed of anti-white, and anti-Semitic diatribes, only serving to exacerbate "black rage." Obama also discusses his introduction to Reverend Jeremiah Wright, minister of the Trinity United Church of Christ in Chicago, whose radical views and affiliation with the presidential candidate were to plague Obama through his 2008 campaign. In fact, one of Wright's sermons, entitled "The Audacity of Hope," was to become the title of Obama's second book."It was into my father's image, the black man, son of Africa, that I'd packed all the attributes I sought in myself, the attributes of Martin and Malcolm, Dubois and Mandela."[4] One issue that Obama discussed and fretted over was gun violence in the city of Chicago. It is still an issue today. (In 2018, 561 homicides were reported in Chicago.) *Dreams from my Father* was republished in 2004, the year Obama won the U.S. Senate Democratic Primary in Illinois.

AWARDS

Dreams from My Father received several notable accolades. The audio version of Obama's book received a Grammy in 2006. The NAACP presented its Image Award for Outstanding Literature in 2007. In 2009, the book received the British Book award for Best Biography. Robert McCrum, in an online article that appeared in the

Guardian in 2016, proclaimed *Dreams From my Father* as number five on the list of 100 Best Non- Fiction Books of All Time.[5]

THE AUDACITY OF HOPE (2006)

The title of Obama's second book, published in 2006, as mentioned previously, was taken from a sermon given by the Reverend Jeremiah Wright of Chicago and served to outline his beliefs, both political as well as social. The body of this work contained material taken from Obama's keynote speech delivered at the 2004 Democratic National Convention. *The Audacity of Hope* became a bestseller and was on *The New York Times* list for thirty weeks. It was on the Amazon.com list as well. An endorsement by Oprah Winfrey helped promote the book. The audio version of the book earned a 2008 Grammy Award for Best Spoken-Word Album. Obama drew large crowds at his book-signing events. Three months after the book's publication, he announced that he was going to run for president in 2008.

From the opening pages, Obama makes clear that he is conscious of his heritage and unsure of his place in the world. "I can't help but view the American experience through the lens of a black man of mixed heritage, forever mindful of how generations of people who looked like me were subjugated and stigmatized…"[6]

Obama believed that there should be a happy medium between capitalism and a government-run economy, a consensus to satisfy the needs and wants of most Americans. "… Examples of where we can break free of our current political stalemate: places where, in the tradition of Hamilton and Lincoln, we can invest in our infrastructure and our people; ways that we can begin to modernize and rebuild the social contract that FDR first stitched together in the middle of the last century."[7] On the other hand, Herbert Hoover, in his book, *A Challenge to Liberty,* warns the American people of the evils of FDR's New Deal and that such policies would lead the country down the path to blatant socialism.

Obama wrote of his political philosophy that was centered on his ideology. "…My fellow legislators' speech helps underscore one of the differences between ideology and values: Values are faithfully applied to the facts before us, while ideology overrides whatever facts call theory into question."[8]

REVIEWS OF *THE AUDACITY OF HOPE*

Obama's second book received many accolades, mostly positive. Peter Preston of *The Guardian* wrote: "*The Audacity of Hope* invites sterner scrutiny than your average political potboiler. It is a presidential calling card. It may be all our futures."[9] Preston went on to write: "Tired of confrontations between neocons and old-style liberals locked in a time warp? Discover the joys of compromise and intelligent discussion with Obama: make positive consensus your theme for the 21st century."

Obama was markedly honest in his assessment of this work. He observed: "I offer no unifying theory of American government, nor do these pages provide a manifesto for action complete with charts and graphs, timetables and ten-point plans." The *Audacity of Hope* included conversations on the campaign trail when Obama ran for the US Senate from Illinois. It developed the topic "How we might begin the process of changing our politics and our civic life."[10]

The New York Times review was also quite laudatory. Pulitzer Prize-winning critic Michiko Kakutami wrote: "Mr. Obama's new book *The Audacity of Hope* ...is much more of a political document. Portions of the volume read like outtakes from a stump speech, and the bulk of it is devoted to laying out Mr. Obama's policy positions on a host of issues from education to health care to the war in Iraq."[11]

Other reviews were not so flattering. "An advance review in *Publishers Weekly* had dismissed the book as a "sonorous manifesto" offering muddled, uninspiring proposals that represented only "tepid Clintonism."[12]

The Audacity of Hope created a great deal of media attention that led a reporter from a Chicago newspaper wondering out loud why Mr. Obama should wait to announce his candidacy for President of the United States. It seemed that was the direction that the senator was heading.

Peter Firstbrook, author of *The Obamas*, observed: "For anybody who has read his (Obama's) books, in *Dreams* and *Audacity*, it is clear that President Obama is very conscious of his mixed heritage, and that as a young man he was unsure of his place in a multicultural world."[13]

Obama's cachet spread beyond the borders of the United States after he became president. Here is a segment of an interview with Russian media:

"What gave you the Audacity of Hope?"

Obama: "You know when I think back, I think my mother was such an important figure in my life. I grew up without a father in the household, but my mother gave me love and support and confidence that I could do anything I set out my mind to doing. And I think that if there's one person who is responsible for success, it would have to be her."[14]

The Audacity of Hope has been translated into many languages, including Italian, Spanish, French, German and Croatian.

OF THEE I SING: A LETTER TO MY DAUGHTERS (2010)

Barack Obama wrote this inspirational book to his daughters, Sasha and Malia, while he was still in the White House. Illustrated by well-known artist Loren Long, this forty-page illustrated work speaks to the beliefs that thirteen great Americans have championed and that Obama would like to instill them in his daughters. The thirteen individuals he has chosen are: George Washington, Abraham Lincoln, Martin Luther King Jr., Neil Armstrong, Sitting Bull, Cesar Chavaz, Billie Holiday, Maya Lin, Albert Einstein, Georgia O'Keeffe, Jackie Robinson, Helen Keller, and Jane Addams. Those included on this list exhibited the human potential that Obama believed helped to make America a great nation. The list transcended gender, race, and religion.

In 2017 President Obama, along with his wife, Michelle, published *Be Vigilant, But Not Afraid.* This work is a compilation of farewell speeches given by the couple, as they were about to leave the White House. It served as a written victory lap highlighting their eight years in office. Proceeds from the sale of this book were to be donated to The American Civil Liberties Union (ACLU) and the National Association for the Advancement of Colored People (NAACP).

WHAT IS OBAMA'S NEXT WRITING PROJECT?

At the time of this book's publication, former President Barack Obama is writing his memoirs. He has signed a publishing agreement with Simon & Schuster, and it is anticipated that the book will be available for the public some time in 2020. Because Obama has a reputation as a cogent and thoughtful writer, this book is widely anticipated.

Barack Obama is a young and gifted writer. Readers of presidential literature both in the United States and around the world should have more opportunities to read his work in the future.

(Library of Congress Photographic and Print Division, LC-DIG-ppbd-00607)

Donald J. Trump
Born: June 14, 1946- New York, New York
45th President
Term: 2017-
Wives: Ivana Zelnickova, Marla Maples, Melania Knauss
Political Party: Republican
Undergraduate College: University of Pennsylvania

Donald Trump's background as an author is unique in many respects. Even though his name is listed as the author of at least 10 books, Meredith McIver, who was a Trump Organization staff member, is given credit in a number of the publications.

Unlike books written by many of his predecessors in the Oval Office, Trump's books that were written early in his career have nothing to do with politics or government. They are primarily focused on his acumen as a shrewd businessman and real estate developer. He also wrote a book about how to improve your golf game. Not until the book *The America We Deserve* does Trump begin to examine the political landscape in the United States. With that book, written in 2000 with author Dave Shiflett, Trump was preparing for a presidential run as a third-party candidate on the Reform Party ticket. It was here that his immigration policy was taking shape. "A liberal policy of immigration may seem to reflect confidence and generosity. But our current laxness toward illegal immigration shows a recklessness and disregard for those who live here legally."

THE ART OF THE DEAL (1987)

Trump's first book, *The Art of the Deal*, published in 1987, became a best seller. The book was at the top of *The New York Times* Bestseller list for 134 weeks. Recent accounts indicate that there have been over one million copies sold in hardback and paperback editions. The book was readily available in all of Trump's Atlantic City casinos. There has been a great deal of controversy about the role that author Tony Schwartz played in the writing. Schwartz has alleged, on several occasions, that he alone wrote the book and has said that he regrets being a part of the project.

The Art of the Deal attracted readers on multiple levels. Trump spells out his recipe for success in business and boasts of his acumen in deal making. He devotes pages to discussing his acquisition of the Commodore Hotel at Grand Central Terminal, his first significant real estate deal in New York. He also recounted his dealing with the City of New York to revitalize the Wollman ice skating rink in Central Park. Trump provides his plans for changing the face of the New York City skyline, especially with the completion of his iconic Trump Tower building on Fifth Avenue, his residence in the city. Trump also devotes pages to his acquisition of the USFL (United States Football League) franchise, New Jersey Generals, and his lawsuit against the National Football League. The USFL ultimately folded. Trump believes that his deal-making skills are innate. He remarks: "More than anything else I think deal making is an ability you're born with." *The Art of the Deal* became a best seller for a second time upon Trump's election as 45th President of the United States.

THE AMERICA WE DESERVE (WITH DONALD SHIFLETT, 2000)

The America We Deserve, published by Renaissance Books, provided readers a first glimpse of the politics of Donald Trump. He has a vision for this country and its future. Trump defines his policy beliefs on issues such as the education system, foreign policy—especially in dealing with China, Russia, North Korea, and Israel—job stimulation and immigration. He also writes about crime and terrorism. Readers can begin to see a metamorphosis from Trump the businessman to Trump the 45th President of the United States.

TRUMP 101: THE WAY TO SUCCESS. DONALD J TRUMP WITH MEREDITH MCIVER (HOBOKEN, NEW JERSEY, JOHN WILEY & SONS, INC. 2007)

The author of the book's Foreword, Michael Sexton, at that time was president of Trump University. It is unclear whether this was a text that was part of a course offered by the university or in some way a required reading for its students. Trump University was founded in 2004 and ceased operations in 2010. In 2016, a federal judge approved a $25 million settlement with students who said they had been duped by Trump University. The copyright to this book, is attributed to Trump University.

Trump utilizes his well-documented experiences as a businessman, real estate mogul and reality-TV show icon to offer advice and witticisms to those who wish to succeed in the competitive world of business. The book is filled with photos of Trump and a number of his projects. There are excerpts from his daily planning schedule, indicating just how busy he is. Also included are questions sent to the Trump University blog. At the conclusion of each chapter is a section entitled "Coach Trump- Make it happen in your life." Here the reader will find bulleted tidbits of wisdom based on Trump's experiences in the business world. Trump liked to use short chapters, usually three pages or so. *Trump 101* has 33 chapters plus an appendix.

NEVER GIVE UP. HOW I TURNED MY BIGGEST CHALLENGES INTO SUCCESS (WITH MEREDITH MCIVER 2008

In *Never Give Up*, Trump provides great detail about how he was approached by Mark Burnett with the idea for *The Apprentice* reality television show. He admits that his advisers at the time did not think it was a good idea. Even Trump felt that the project would take too much time away from his other business dealings. But he noted: "If I had listened to everyone, *The Apprentice* never would have happened."[15] At the end of each chapter is a highlighted paragraph titled: "Coach Trump—Make it Happen in Your Life."

Trump provided this bit of philosophy to his readers. "Let your passion for your work carry you through all the setbacks they can throw at you. Be it wind, water, resignations, scandals, whatever— you can prevail."[16] At the end of the book are several pages of advertisements encouraging the reader to sign up and enroll in Trump University.

DONALD J. TRUMP- THINK LIKE A CHAMPION (WRITTEN WITH MEREDITH MCIVER, 2009)

This work is mostly a repeat of some of the same anecdotes and phrases used in *Trump 101*. However, I did find this passage of interest. When asked about the 2008 election of Barack Obama, Trump said:

He (Obama) will simply have to be great, which he has a very good chance of being. What he has done is amazing. The fact that he accomplished what he has, in one year against great odds, is truly phenomenal. If someone had asked me if a black man or woman could become president, I would have said yes, but not yet. Barack Obama proved determination combined with opportunity and intelligence can make things happen in an exceptional way.[17]

TIME TO GET TOUGH- MAKING AMERICA #1 AGAIN (2011)

In reviewing President Trump's first term in office, readers of this book, published in 2011, will immediately note the consistency in his message. This book was to be the kick-start to a potential bid for the presidency in 2012, this time as a candidate for the Republican nomination, not as a third-party candidate. Trump devotes an entire chapter to his desire and the necessity to repeal Obamacare. He also points out how America has been taken advantage of by China and how a better dealmaker (like him) would be able to obtain a more favorable trade balance with China. Trump takes every opportunity throughout the book to berate the administration of Barack Obama and implores his readers to elect someone else and deny the incumbent president a second term.

Trump goes on to reiterate, in no uncertain terms, that America is a capitalist country; business owners are integral in keeping the economy going, hiring employees, paying taxes— again chiding Obama on his position of raising taxes on the wealthy. Additionally, this book also foreshadows his current position on the issue of immigration, as Trump rails against America's current policies and how the government has been mishandling illegal immigration. He also stresses the importance of ridding the country of its dependence on OPEC and expanding domestic opportunities for fossil fuels.

Trump had second thoughts about running at that time. He said: "After considerable deliberation and reflection, I have decided not to pursue the office of the presidency. This decision does not come easily or without regret, especially when my potential candidacy continues to be validated by ranking at the top of the Republican contenders in polls across the country." This was at a time when Trump's TV show *The Celebrity Apprentice* was quite popular, and his businesses appeared to be successful.

Unlike many of Trump's other books, *Time to Get Tough* does not display Meredith McIver's name on the cover as a co-author or contributor. However, in the acknowledgments at the back of the book Trump thanks Rhona Graff, Michael Cohen, Kacey Kennedy, Thuy Colayco, and Meredith McIver for their work. In attempting to determine the provenance of the work and identifying who provided the research for all of the footnotes, one can assume that these staff members of the Trump Organization were instrumental in writing *Time to Get Tough.*

CRIPPLED AMERICA: HOW TO MAKE AMERICA GREAT AGAIN (2015)

Crippled America was a significant deviation from Trump's other works that lauded his business prowess and financial successes while offering advice to "students" enrolled at Trump University. This book is the politically driven work that helped launch Donald Trump's 2016 presidential campaign. The book was retitled "*Great Again: How to Fix our Crippled America* and was re-issued in July 2016. In this work Trump attacks the mainstream media, lays out his platform on immigration reform and attempts to establish and solidify his conservative base. He wrote:

"I am not going to play the same game politicians have been playing for decades—all talk, no action, while special interests and lobbyists dictate our laws. I am shaking up the establishment on both sides of the political aisles because I can't be bought. I want to bring America back, to make it great and prosperous again, and to be sure we are respected by our allies and feared by our adversaries."[18]

In *Crippled America* Donald Trump also signals what is to become a hallmark of his presidency: using social media, particularly Twitter, to make often outrageous statements. "Sometimes I make outrageous comments and give them what they want—viewers and readers—in order to make a point."[19]

There is reason to believe that another book is in the works that will be used to launch Trump's re-election bid in 2020. Beyond that, given his past publishing history, the reading public can expect to see Trump's memoirs and possibly other books about his leadership style and handling of government policies and events in the coming years. (Author's note: I contacted the White House Press Office in February 2020 to inquire about a possible forthcoming book. As of the date of publication, there has been no reply.)

---

[1] Barack Obama. *Dreams From my Father: A Story of Race and Inheritance.*
(New York: Three Rivers Press, 2004).
[2] Ibid., p. 437.
[3] David J. Garrow. Rising Star: The Making of Barack Obama.
(New York: HarperCollins Publishers, 2017). 511-512.
[4] Obama, *Dreams*. p. 220.
[5] (Guardian online 2/29/16. Accessed 4/25/19).
[6] Barack Obama. *The Audacity of Hope: Thoughts on Reclaiming the American Dream.*
(New York: Crown Publishers, 2006). 10.
[7] *Ibid.*, p. 159.
[8] *Ibid.*, p. 59
[9] From Peter Preston in *The Guardian* on line April 28, 2007. Accessed May 8, 2019.
[10] Obama. *Audacity*. p. 9.
[11] "Obama's Foursquare Politics with dab of Dijon," *The New York Times*. 10/17/06 retrieved 10/30/19).
[12] Garrow, p. 1004.
[13] Peter Firstbrook. *The Obamas*
(New York: Crown Publishers, 2010), 2.
[14] Tass/ Rossiya TV July 2, 2009
[15] *Ibid.*, p. 11.
[16] Donald J. Trump. *Never Give Up: How I Turned my Biggest Challenges Into Success.*
(New Jersey: John Wiley and Sons, 2008). 17.
[17] Donald J. Trump. *Think Like a Champion.*
(New York: Vanguard Press, 2009). 1-2.
[18] Donald J. Trump. *Crippled America: How to Make America Great Again*
(New York: Simon & Schuster, 2015). 17.
[19] *Ibid.*, p. 19

CONCLUSION

The literature of America's presidents transcends four centuries of our nation's history. The nature of the men has changed. So too have many of their ideals. From the atlas that described one of this country's original states in detail, to the book-length campaign promotional literature of today, our commanders-in-chief have seen fit to shower the public with more than 150 books with, undoubtedly, more to come. Many of these works became bestsellers as the reading public demanded to know about the personal lives, successes, and failures of these men who have held the office of President of the United States. In the current century, social media has served to magnify the impact of the writings of our country's leaders.

The 44 men who have risen to the office of President have come from all walks of life. Some were generals; others were farmers. Many of them were lawyers. The memoirs of these men have often served as documents of revisionism, meant to burnish their administrations and provide a foundation for a legacy that will ultimately find its way to their Presidential Libraries and Museums. It has also made a number of them rich.

The Quinnipiac Polling organization has never conducted a survey to see if the books written by presidential candidates made a difference on Election Day. Most people don't seem to believe they have, but that will probably not deter future candidates from putting their thoughts and ideas on paper. In any given year, between 600,000 and one million books are published in the United States, all hoping to grab the reader's attention. Presidents or presidential hopefuls write only a portion of them.

The final musical number in act two of the smash-hit Broadway musical *Hamilton* is titled "Who Lives, Who Dies, Who Tells Your Story." Some of our former presidents will strive to tell their stories through their own lens. Many university professors and presidential historians will also be ready to write their own interpretations of our chief executives. The final arbiters, however, will be the reading public. What do we want to remember about our presidents? Do we want to preserve the detailed accounts of the Civil War? Should we remember the contributions of the diverse immigrant groups who helped shape America? Or do we need to be reminded of the ongoing struggle to preserve our democracy from threats both foreign and domestic?

Presidential literature is a reflection of our American culture and society. In many cases it identifies what is important to us as a nation. We as a nation should never stop reading and our leaders need to continue to provide us with their thoughts and ideas that are the fabric of our country and a mirror of its history.

Appendix I

Selected Books by U.S. Presidents

John Adams
Thought in Government Applicable to the Present State of the American Colonies

The Writings of John Adams

John Quincy Adams
Publicola

Letters on Freemasonry

Jimmy Carter
The Craftsmanship of Jimmy Carter

Full Life: Reflections at Ninety

A Call to Action: Women, Religion, Violence, and Power

NIV Lessons from Life Bible: Personal Reflections with Jimmy Carter

Through the Year with Jimmy Carter: 366 Daily Meditations from the 39th President

White House Diary

We can Have Peace in the Holy Land: A Plan That Will Work

A Remarkable Mother

Beyond the White House: Waging Peace, Fighting Disease, Building Hope

Palestine Peace not Apartheid

Sharing Good Times

The Hornet's Nest: A Novel of the Revolutionary War

The Nobel Peace Prize Lecture

Christmas in Plains: Memories (illustrated by Amy Carter)

An Hour Before Daylight: Memories of a Rural Boyhood

The Virtues of Aging

Sources of Strength: Meditations on Scripture for a Living Faith

The Little Baby Snoogle-Fleejer (illustrated by Amy Carter)

Always a Reckoning and Other Poems

Talking Peace: A Vision for the Next Generation

Turning Points: A Candidate, a State, and a Nation Come of Age

An Outdoor Journal: Adventures and Reflections

Everything to Gain: Making the Most of the Rest of Your Life (with Rosalynn Carter)

The Blood of Abraham: Insights into the Middle East

Keeping Faith: Memoirs of a President

A Government as Good as Its People

Why Not the Best?

Faith: A Journey for all

Bill Clinton

Back to Work

My Life

Giving

Between Hope and History

The President is Missing (With James Patterson)

Dwight D. Eisenhower

Crusade in Europe

Mandate for Change

At Ease: Stories I Tell to Friends

Ulysses S. Grant
Personal Memoirs

Herbert Hoover
American Individualism

The Challenge to Liberty

The Ordeal of Woodrow Wilson

Principles of Mining

The Economics of Mining

Executive Personnel Balance Sheet

Memoirs of Herbert Hoover (three volumes)

The New Day

On Growing Up: Letter to American Boys and Girls

The Problems of Lasting Peace (With Hugh Gibson)

The Basis of Lasting Peace (With Hugh Gibson)

Prefaces to Peace

A New South Dakota History

The Chitimaca People

Freedom Betrayed

America's First Crusade

Thomas Jefferson
Notes on the State of Virginia

The Jefferson Bible

Autobiography of Thomas Jefferson

John F. Kennedy
Why England Slept

Profiles in Courage

A Nation of Immigrants

To Turn the Tide

The Strategy of Peace

The Burden and the Glory

Richard Nixon
Six Crises

Leaders

No More Vietnams

In the Arena

The Real War

Beyond Peace

1999 Victory Without War

Seize the Moment: America's Challenge in a One-Superpower World

Barack Obama
The Audacity of Hope

Dreams from My Father

Of Thee I Sing

Be Vigilant but Not Afraid: The Farewell Speeches of Barack Obama and Michelle Obama

Theodore Roosevelt
The Winning of the West

The Rough Riders

The Naval War of 1812

Hunting Trips of a Ranchman

Thomas Hart Benton

Gouverneur Morris

Ranch Life and the Hunting Trail

The Wilderness Hunter

Hero Tales from American History (With Henry Cabot Lodge)

American Ideals and Other Essays

Life of Oliver Cromwell

The Strenuous Life

Outdoor Pastimes of an American Hunter

Good Hunting

True Americanism

African Game Trails

African and European Addresses

The New Nationalism

Realizable Ideals

Conservation of Womanhood and Childhood

History as Literature and Other Essays

Theodore Roosevelt (an autobiography)

Progressive Principles

Life Histories of African Game Animals (with Edmund Heller)

Through the Brazilian Wilderness

Stories of the Great West

America and the World War

A Booklover's Holidays in the Open

Fear God and Take Your Own Part

The Foes of our Own Household

The Great Adventure (Studies in Nationalism)

National Strength and International Duty

Theodore Roosevelt's Letters to His Children

Donald Trump

Trump: The Art of the Deal

Trump 101: The Way to Success

Think Like a Champion

Trump: How to get Rich

The Art of the Comeback

The America We Deserve

Great Again

Time to Get Tough

Midas Touch (with Robert T. Kiyosaki)

Trump: Think Big

Trump: The Best Golf Advice I Ever Received

Trump: Think Like a Billionaire

Trump: The Best Real Estate Advice I Ever Received

Woodrow Wilson

Study of Public Administration

Constitutional Government

Congressional Government

On Being Human

The New Freedom

A History of the American People (five volumes)

George Washington: A Life

Division and Reunion 1829-1889

APPENDIX II

The Carter Center

With the establishment of the Jimmy Carter Presidential Library and Museum in Atlanta and his being awarded the Nobel Peace Prize in 2002, Jimmy and Rosalynn Carter established the Carter Center. "The Carter Center, in partnership with Emory University, is guided by a fundamental commitment to human rights and the alleviation of human suffering. It seeks to prevent and resolve conflicts, enhance freedom and democracy, and improve health. It boasts an honor roll of members identified as the Council of Freely elected heads of government."[1] (Carter Center website)

- The Center emphasizes action and measurable results. Based on careful research and analysis, it is prepared to take timely action on important and pressing issues.
- The Center seeks to break new ground and not duplicate the effective efforts of others.
- The Center addresses difficult problems in difficult situations and recognizes the possibility of failure as an acceptable risk.
- The Center is nonpartisan, actively seeks complementary partnerships and works collaboratively with other organizations from the highest levels of government to local communities.
- The Center believes that people can improve their own lives when provided with the necessary skills, knowledge, and access to resources."

(From Carter Center website cartercenter.org.)[1]

---

1 Carter Center website

APPENDIX III

Presidents Without a College Degree

One of the issues raised in this book was whether a college education helped to make a better writer of a future president. While the results may be inconclusive, there are nine U.S. Presidents who did not have an undergraduate college degree.

George Washington
Martin Van Buren
Zachary Taylor
Millard Fillmore
Andrew Jackson
Abraham Lincoln
Andrew Johnson
Grover Cleveland
Harry Truman

FOR FURTHER READING

Adams, John. *Thoughts on Government Applicable to the Present State of the American Colonies.*
Philadelphia: John Dunlap, 1776.

Astor, Gerald. *Presidents at War from Truman to Bush*
Hoboken, New Jersey: John Wiley and Sons, 2006.

Berg, A. Scott. *Wilson*
New York: G.P. Putnam's Sons, 2013.

Bestor, Arthur; Mearns, David C.; Daniels, Jonathan. *Three Presidents and Their Books*
Urbana, Illinois: University of Illinois Press, 1955.

Brinkley, Douglas. *The Unfinished Presidency: Jimmy Carter's Journey Beyond the White House*. New York: Viking Press, 1999.

Bush, George H.W. *All the Best: My Life in Letters and Other Writings*
New York: Scribner, 2013.

Bush, George W. *On God and Country*: *The President Speaks Out About Faith, Principle and Patriotism*
Longwood, Florida: Allegiance Press, 2004.

Bush, George W. *41- A Portrait of My Father*
New York: Crown Publishers, 2014.

Bush, George W. *Decision Points*
New York: Crown Publishers, 2010.

Bush, George W. *Portraits of Courage*: *A Commander in Chief's Tribute to America's Warriors*. New York: Crown Publishing Group, 2017.

Bush, George W. and Herskowitz, Michael. *A Charge to Keep* New York: William Morrow and Company, Inc., *1999.*

Carter, Jimmy. *Always a Reckoning and Other Poems* New York: Time Books, *1995.*

Carter, Jimmy. *Beyond the White House: Waging Peace, Fighting Disease, Building Hope* New York: Simon & Schuster, 2007.

Carter, Jimmy. *An Hour Before Daylight* New York: Simon & Schuster, 2001.

Carter, Jimmy. *A Full Life: Reflections at Ninety (Also in audio)* New York: Simon & Schuster, 2015.

Carter, Jimmy. *Faith: A Journey for all* New York: Simon & Schuster, 2018.

Carter, Jimmy. *The Hornet's N*est New York: Simon & Schuster, 2003.

Carter, Jimmy. *Palestine Peace Not Apartheid.* New York: Simon & Schuster, 2006.

Carter, Jimmy. *Our Endangered Values: America's Moral Crisis.* New York: Simon & Schuster, 2005.

Carter, Jimmy. *Why Not the Best- The First Fifty Years* Fayetteville, Arkansas: University of Arkansas Press, 1996. (revised edition of original book- edited by Douglass Brinkley)

Chernow, Ron. *Grant* New York: Penguin Random House, 2017.

Clinton, Bill. *Between Hope and Happiness* New York: Random House, 1996.

Clinton, Bill. *Giving: How Each of us can Change the World*
New York: Alfred A. Knopf, 2007.

Clinton, Bill. *My Life.*
New York: Alfred A. Knopf, 2005.

Conason, Joe. *Man of the World: The Further Endeavors of Bill Clinton*
New York: Simon & Schuster, 2016.

Eisenhower, Dwight D. *Crusade in Europe*
New York: Doubleday and Company, 1948.

Eisenhower, Dwight D. *Mandate for Change* 1953-1956.
Garden City: Doubleday and Company, Inc. 1963.

Eizenstat, Stuart E. *President Carter: The White House Years*
New York: St. Martin's Press, 2018.

Ellis, Joseph J. *American Sphinx: The Character of Thomas Jefferson*
New York: Vintage Press, 1998.

Firstbrook, Peter. *The Obamas*
New York: Crown Publishers, 2010.

Garrow, David J. *Rising Star: The Making of Barack Obama*
New York: HarperCollins Publishers, *2017.*

Gibbs, Nancy and Duffy, Michael. *The Presidents Club- Inside the World's Most Exclusive Fraternity.*
New York: Simon & Schuster, 2012.

Goodwin, Doris Kearns. *The Bully Pulpit: Theodore Roosevelt, William Howard Taft, and the Golden Age of Journalism*
New York: Simon & Schuster, 2013.

Grant, Ulysses S. *Personal Memoirs.* (Caleb Carr, editor)

New York: Modern Library, 1999.

Greenstein, Fred I. *The Presidential Difference: Leadership Style from FDR to Clinton.*
New York: The Free Press, 2000.

Harbaugh, William Henry. *The Life and Times of Theodore Roosevelt*
New York: Collier Books, 1961.

Hoover, Herbert. *American Individualism (1922) and The Challenge to Liberty (1934)*
West Branch, Iowa: Herbert Hoover Presidential Library Association, 1989.

Hoover, Herbert, *The Ordeal of Woodrow Wilson*
New York: McGraw-Hill Book Company, Inc., 1958.

Jefferson, Thomas. *Notes on the State of Virginia*
William Peden, ed.
New York: W.W. Norton and Company*, 1982.*

Kearns Goodwin, Doris. *The Bully Pulpit: Theodore Roosevelt, William Howard Taft and the Gilded Age of Journalism*
New York: Simon & Schuster, 2013

Kennedy, John F. *Why England Slept*
New York: Wilfred Funk, Inc., 1940.

Kennedy, John F. *Profiles in Courage*
New York: Harper Brothers, 1956.

Kennedy, John F. *A Nation of Immigrants*
New York: Harper Perennial, 2018.

Korda, Michael. *Ike*
New York: HarperCollins, 2007.

Malone, Dumas. *Jefferson and His Time Vol. VI-The Sage of Monticello.*
Boston: Little, Brown, and Company, 1981.

Matviko, John W. ed. *The American President in Popular Culture*
Westport, Conn: Greenwood Press, 2005.

Maynard, W. Barksdale. *Woodrow Wilson: Princeton to the Presidency*
New Haven, Yale University Press, 2008.

Miller, Nathan. *Theodore Roosevelt- a Life*
New York: William Morrow, 1992.

McCullough, David. *The American Spirit: Who we are and What we Stand For*
New York: Simon & Schuster, 2017.

Moore, Kathyrn. *The American President: A Complete History*
New York: Fall River Press, 2007.

Nixon, Richard M. *No More Vietnams*
New York: Arbor House, 1985.

Nixon, Richard M. *Leaders: Profiles and Reminiscences of Men Who Have Shaped the Modern World.*
New York: Warner Books, 1982.

Obama, Barack. *Dreams From my Father: A Story of Race and Inheritance (also in audio)*
New York: Three Rivers Press (paperback), 2004.

Obama, Barack. *The Audacity of Hope: Thoughts on Reclaiming the American Dream*
New York: Crown Publishers, 2006.

Perry, Mark. *Grant and Twain: The Story of a Friendship that Changed America*
New York: Random House, 2004.

Roosevelt, Theodore. *The Naval War of 1812.*
New York: The Modern Library, (1999 edition)

Roosevelt, Theodore. *History as Literature and Other Essays.*
New York: Charles Scribner, 1913.

Roosevelt, Theodore. *The Great Adventure*
New York: Charles Scribner's Sons, 1919.
Samet, Elizabeth, ed. *Annotated Memoirs of Ulysses S. Grant*
New York: Liveright Publishing Corp, 2019.

Sandler, Martin, ed. *The Letters of John F. Kennedy*
New York: Bloomsbury Press, 2013.
(note: correspondence between JFK and Eleanor Roosevelt as well as Khrushchev, Jackie Robinson, Sir Winston Churchill, Rev. Billy Graham)

Schick, Frank L.; Schick, Renee; Mark Carroll. *Records of the Presidency: Presidential Papers and Libraries from Washington to Reagan.*
Phoenix, Arizona: Oryx Press, 1989.

Skidmore, Max J. *After the White House: Former Presidents as Private Citizens.*
New York: Palgrave MacMillan, 2004.

Taylor, Tim. *The Book of Presidents*
New York: Arno Press, 1972.

Troy, Tevi. *What Jefferson Read, Ike Watched, and Obama Tweeted*
Washington, D.C.: Regnery Publishing, Inc., 2013.

Truman, Harry S. and Acheson, Dean. *Affection and Trust: The Personal Correspondence of Harry S. Truman and Dean Acheson.*

New York: Alfred A Knopf, 2010.

Trump, Donald J. *Crippled America: How to Make America Great Again*
New York: Simon & Schuster, 2015.

Trump, Donald J. *Never Give Up: How I Turned My Biggest Challenges Into Success*
New Jersey: John Wiley and Sons, 2008.

Trump, Donald J. with McIver, Meredith, *Think Like a Champion: An Informal Education in Business and Life.*
New York: Vanguard Press, 2009.

Trump, Donald J. with McIver, Meredith, *Trump 101*
Hoboken, New Jersey: John Wiley and Sons, 2007 Trump University.

Trump, Donald J. *Time to Get Tough: Making America #1 Again*
Washington, DC: Regnery Publishing, Inc., 2011.

Wilson, Woodrow. *Congressional Government: A Study in American Politics*
Cambridge, Massachusetts: The Riverside Press, (original copyright 1885).

Wilson, Woodrow. *Constitutional Government of the United States*
New York: Columbia University Press, 1964. (original copyright 1911)

Wilson, Woodrow. *Division and Reunion 1829-1889*
New York: Longmans, Green, and Co., 1898.

Wilson, Woodrow. *The New Freedom: A Call for The Emancipation of the Generous Energies of a People.* New York: Doubleday, Page and Company, 1913.

Wilson, Woodrow. *A History of the American People* (five volumes)

New York: Harper and Brothers Publishers, 1901.

Afterword

In his thought-provoking book on presidential leaderships style, *The Presidential Difference,* Princeton Professor emeritus Fred Greenstein believed that, of primary importance, a president must be proficient as a public communicator. The question arises as to whether the best presidents were the good communicators and was that quality evident in their writings.

More recently, C-SPAN gathered a panel of presidential historians and scholars to identify qualities of presidential leadership. They developed a list of ten such qualities. They include: "Public persuasion, crisis leadership, economic management, moral authority, international relations, administrative skills, relations with congress, vision/setting an agenda, pursued equal justice for all, and performance within the context of the times." (From *The Presidents*: *Noted Historians Rank America's Best and Worst Chief Executives* by Brian Lamb, Susan Swain and C-SPAN. New York, Public Affairs, 2019.)

Former President Jimmy Carter once spoke of the "man and the moment coming together" as a presage to his election. If that is the case, then very little of a president's literature can be attributed to his success at the polls. Many of Carter's post presidential writings are evangelical in nature; and while he could have followed in his father's footsteps and run the family business, while he could have remained in the navy and commanded a nuclear submarine, it would not have been beyond reason to see him follow his sister, Ruth Carter Stapleton as a Christian evangelist. For Theodore Roosevelt and John F. Kennedy, a career in journalism was a real possibility, especially for Roosevelt. Literary attributes of a candidate, however, have not foreshadowed a successful presidency. Innate writing skills, university training, and marketing strategies may get a book to the top of the bestseller list but there are a myriad of other factors that go into the making of a great presidency.

ABOUT THE AUTHOR

Jeff Margolis is an educator, author and lecturer and has spent much of his academic career working with teachers and future teachers. He was elected to the Rowan University Wall of Fame on three occasions for his work with college students. He is the author of several books, most notably *Violence in Sports* and *Teen Crime Wave*. He was also a contributor to the *Encyclopedia of New Jersey* and has served on the editorial board of the American Association for Employment in Education Annual Handbook for Teachers. He has presented papers at numerous academic conferences around the country and served as an advisor for several textbooks. Margolis is currently a member of the board of governors of The Press Club of Southwest Florida, and a member of the Naples Council on World Affairs and Friends of the Library. In Florida Mr. Margolis has lectured at the Renaissance Academy, Collier County Library, Holocaust Museum of Southwest Florida and Florida Southwest State College. Jeff lives in Florida with his wife, Ida. Together they enjoy traveling around the country visiting museums, libraries and historical sites relating to US Presidents.

INDEX